William Mc Intyre

1·5·05.

The Letters of
Harry Tartt

The Light and Bitter Years

EBURY
PRESS

First published in Great Britain in 2000

1 3 5 7 9 10 8 6 4 2

Ebury Press
Random House, 20 Vauxhall Bridge Road, London SW1V 2SA

Random House Australia Pty Limited
20 Alfred Street, Milsons Point, Sydney, New South Wales 2061,
Australia

Random House New Zealand Limited
18 Poland Road, Glenfield, Auckland 10, New Zealand

Random House South Africa (Pty) Limited
Endulini, 5A Jubilee Road, Parktown 2193, South Africa

The Random House Group Limited Reg. No 954009

www.randomhouse.co.uk

A CIP catalogue record for this book is available from the
British Library

ISBN 0 09 187459 9

Design by Dan Newman/Perfect Bound

Jacket Photographs Matthew May

Photographs of Todd Carty, Terry Wogan, Derek Jameson,
Edwina Currie, Ned Sherrin, June Brown © BBC; photograph of
Ant & Dec © Zenith Entertainment plc; photographs of Ian
McCaskill & Bill Giles © The Met Office; photograph of Pat
Coombes courtesy Pat Coombes; photograph of Robert Kilroy-
Silk © Kilroy; photograph of John Altman © Nicholas Bowman.

Printed in Great Britain by Cambridge University Press

Papers used by Ebury Press are natural, recyclable products
made from wood grown in sustainable forests

I offer thanks to: the staff at The Wavelengths
Library for helping me type on their lovely
computers, and for bravely pulling me out of that
freak electrical fire; Steve McAuliffe, my Link
worker for helping me compile these letters
(sorry for setting the dog on you that time); and
lastly dear old Jeffrey Archer, who helped to
restore my faith in human nature - and believe
me, not many people get to say that!

Harry Tartt
March 2000

26 Baildon Street

Deptford

London

SE8 4BQ.

Your Majesty,

I am A elderly Gent and have few pleasures left in life. However, my dog Bones recentley celebrated his hundreth birthday (in dog years of course). I thought it would be wonderfull if you could send Bones a telagram, and what a tremendoUs way to reveal the light-hearted human side of your nature to sImple folk such as meself.

You're a wonderfull woman m'lady and far from being an outdated institution, I believe the Royals will run and run. God bless you and say hello to your mother (suppose you'll be sending her a telegram soon, ho ho).

I await your reply,

Harry Tartt.

BUCKINGHAM PALACE

16th April, 1996

Dear Mr Tartt,

I am commanded by The Queen to thank you for your letter in which you say that your dog Bones has celebrated his 100th birthday , and you ask if Her Majesty will send a telegram.

I have to explain to you that it is Her Majesty's rule only to send messages of congratulation to her human subjects! This I feel sure you will understand when I tell you of the many letters such as yours that are received.

The Queen thanks you very much for the good wishes you send to her and her family.

Yours sincerely

Mavis Farnham

Lady-in-Waiting

H. Tartt Esq.

26 Baildon Street

Deptford

LONDON SE8 4BQ.

Customer Relations Department

William Hill Bookmakers

Greenside house

50 Station Road

Wood Green

London N22 4TQ.

Dear John Quinn,

Following a discussion in my local pub - which became quite heated - I would like for someone to inform me; is it possible to lay a bet on when the Queen Mother will pass on?

If it is possible, could you tell me the odds on October 1998? (It came to me in a dream you see.)

Awaiting your reply

Harry Tartt.

Customer Relations Department
Helpline 0990 181715

Greenside House, 50 Station Road, Wood Green, London N22 4TP.

PR/AN

23rd May 1996

Mr H. Tartt,
26, Baildon Street,
Deptford,
London,
SE8 4BQ.

Dear Mr Tartt,

Thank you for your recent communication.

We wish to confirm that we do not offer odds any bet that may be considered to be in 'poor taste' (eg. anything involving injury or death).

We trust we have clarified our position on this matter and if we can be of any further assistance please do not hesitate to contact us again.

Yours sincerely,

Paul Roffe
<u>Customer Relations Department</u>

William Hill Organization Limited. Registered Office: Greenside House,
50 Station Road, Wood Green, London N22 4TP. Reg. No. 278208 England

26 Baildon Street
Deptford
London SE8 4BQ.

Dear Diana Farnham (Lady in waiting)

Thanking You for your letter to which I received today.
UnfortunaTely I have some bad News regarding my dog Bones. A
week ago he passed away (three days after his hundredth
Bithday).
To be honesT it wasn't much of a shock as he was all but
blind as A bat and only had three legs Proper.

It would've been nice for him tohave recieved a telegram from
Her Majesty - but that was not to Be. Shame. Still, I have
another Idea which may be you could run past the grand lady.
I am aware that at Westminter Abbey or some such thing, there
is a little graveyard call Poets Corner - how about setting
up a Pets Corner where some peoples animals could be buried?
If this is at all possible could Bones reserve a place? Maybe
it would atone for his disappointment vis a vis the telegram.

Your Loyal subject

Harry Tartt.

26 Baildon street
Deptford
London SE8 4BQ.

Dear Ant and Dec (formerley P.J and Duncan),

I am a seventy-two year old man who thought in the war, but, (and
this might suprise you) I am your greatest fan. I believe that
your comedy has a direct line to the music-HAll. Your act is just
the ticket - cheeky but not rude. Your music's not bad neither.

Can you send a photo to me with the inscription; 'Let's Get Ready
to Rumble.' Cheers lads.

Your greatest fan,

Harry Tartt.

26 Baildon Street
DEptford
London SE8 4BQ.

Dear BRITISH Rail,

As a lonely old man witha loving for trains, I am very UPset at
the high prices charged for rail travel in this country. Now, I
wonder if there is a way of reducing prices WITHOUT punishing the
Great British commuter too much. I think I have an idea - I have
noticed that recentley what with the opening of the Channel
Tunnel and such, there is a lot of foreigners about. Now, why
don't you employ security guards to check peoples' passports and
birth certificates at stations and if found to be not English -
charge them extra! That'd save us long suffering train-users from
subsidising the rail all the time. And what's more - once it's
all privatised you can keep charging them more! Imagine how much
money you could make if they have to make a few connections!
There'd Soon be enough money floating arounD to set upa decent
rail network - with good trains! And friendly staff!

I know this might sound a bit racialist - but let's face it - the
French did next to nothing in the war, the Italians kept chanGing
sides, and the Germans tried to kill us. I reckon it's pay-back
time!

I would appreciate it if you would Let me know what my opinions
mean.   To You.

Yours Sincerely,

Harry Tartt.

SouthEastern

Mr Harry Tartt
26 Baildon Street
Deptford
London
SE8 4BQ

Tel: 0171 620 5555

14 May 1996

Ref: 199848

Dear Mr Tartt,

Thank you for your recent letter.

I was very interested to learn of your suggestion for reducing ticket prices.

Whilst such an idea is not in any way feasible, you may be interested to know that train operators sell a variety of railcards which offer discounts on tickets both countrywide and in the South East. I am enclosing details of these which I hope you will find helpful in reducing the cost of your future rail travel.

Thank you once more for writing. Your letter will not go unheeded, for we are continually striving to improve our services and comments from our customers are always welcome.

Yours sincerely

David Eustace
Passenger Liaison

The South Eastern Train Company

Friars Bridge Court 41-45 Blackfriars Road London SE1 8NZ

The South Eastern Train Company Limited. Registered in England & Wales. No. 3006571. Registered office: Euston House, 24 Eversholt Street, London NW1 1DZ.
A wholly owned subsidiary of the British Railways Board

26 Baildon Street

Deptford

LONDON SE8 4BQ.

Public Relations Officer,

British Meat Manufacturers Association,

19 Cornwall Terrace

LONDON NW1.

Dear Sir or Miss,

First off, comiserations regarding the Beef crisis. Now, what I'm writing to say is - myself and the regulars of the Angry Toad Public House have started up a 'We Back British Beef' campaign. To help us, could you possibly send some stickers and a poster or something?

We're 100 per cent behind you on this (I fought in the war and I'm not about to be licked by the Bosh now)!

Much obliged to you and I await your package.

Harold Tartt.

BMMA
British Meat Manufacturers' Association

18/19 Cornwall Terrace London NW1 4QP   Telephone 0171-935 7980   Facsimile 0171-487 4734   Telex 262027

24 May 1996

Mr H Tartt   LO/2
26 Baildon Street
Deptford
London   SE8 4BQ

Dear Mr Tartt,

Thank you for your letter. I am delighted to hear that the Angry Toad Public
House is backing British beef. The BMMA does not have any particular stickers,
but we enclose a couple that the Meat and Livestock Commission have produced.
You may wish to approach the MLC for further publicity material. The address is:-

Meat and Livestock Commission
PO Box 44
Winterhill House
Snowdon Drive
Milton Keynes   MK6 1AX

Yours sincerely

ELIZABETH M. SUNLEY
Assistant Director

Enc

Director: P.J. Mobsby   Assist
BMMA: A Company Limited

Proud to serve British Beef.

BRITISH
MEAT
Beef

26 Baildon Street

Deptford

LOnDON SE8 4BQ.

Meteorological Office,

London Weather Centre,

127 Clerkenwell Road, EC1.

Dear Ian McCaskell,

A couple of weeks ago you said the weather was going to be dry, so I went out without an umbrella, consequentley it poured down and I got soaked. This led to me getting a very bad cold, which at my age is no laughing matter, especially as I've been feeling a bit down in the dumps since my dog Bones died.

What I want to know is, if you get it wrong, do you get money deducted from your pay?

Seeing as I pay my licence fee I would like a reply this time. (I don't have much money but I've enclosed a stamp for you).

Yours,

Harry Tartt. (Pensioner).

Mr H. Tartt
26 Baildon Street
Deptford
London SE8 EC1

Dear Mr Tartt,

Thank you for your letters.I am sorry you were rained upon-and I was especially sorry to hear about Bones.

A proportion of our wages depend on performance.

Good luck for the future.I enclose your stamp.

yours sincerely,

Ian McCaskill

17/6/92

26 Baildon Street
deptford
London SE8 4BQ.

Metereological Office
London Weather Centre
127 Clerkenwell Road, Ec1.

Dear Ian McCasgill,

Thankyou for your nice letter. I'm sorry if I was a bit kurt with you but maybe I was a bit 'under the weather' (geddit?) After all, I was down with a cold and what not. In fact I now realise that you are not the one I should be having a go at - that should have been reserved for billy Baxter who won my coat in a Queen Mother related bet.

Anyway, your sunny (!) disposession and friendly manner are much appreciated by older folks like meself, unlike Michael fish who I find a little smarmy.

Could you send me a photo of your smiling face and a funny quip purtaining to the weather?

Bye now,

Harry Tartt.

From one tart to another!

Sam MacAulis

26 Baildon Street

deptford

London SE8 4BQ.

Dear Italian Tourist board,

I am an elderly gent who thought in the war. In fact, I was injured in Palermo in 1943 (the details are unimportant). Now, the point is, I would very much like to return to Italy before it is too late.

Would it be possible for you to pay for me to fly to Italy? (and accomdation while there?) It doesn't even have to be Palermo, Rome would do - even Madrid.

I look forward to hearing from you,

Palermo

FLASH GUIDE

ITALIA I AM SORRY TO INFORM YOU THAT WE WON'T BE ABLE TO HELP YOU WITH YOUR REQUEST. PLEASE FIND HERE ENCLOSED SOME GENERAL INFORMATIONS ON SICILY THAT WE HOPE WILL BE USEFUL.

ITALIAN STATE TOURIST BOARD
1 Princes Street · London W1R 8AY
Tel: 071-408 1254 Fax: 071-493 6695

With Compliments

26 Baildon Street
Deptford
London SE8 4BQ.

Conservative Central Office
32 Smith Square
Westminster
London Sw1p 3HH.

Dear Sir/Miss,

I have been taking great pains to back British Beef during this
'war' with Europe - indeed, me and Billy Baxter just the other
day set up a stall on Deptford High Street and munched our way
through thirty beef-burgers dressed in full ceremonial Beefeater
garb!

Yet one thing has disturbed both me and Billy of late - we have
read that the ban on gellatine, tallow,and semen is to be lifted
- all well and good. We have no problems with gellatine and
tallow. What we want to know is, in what products does semen
appear? Is it in beefburgers?

A concerned pensioner,

Harry Tartt.

CONSERVATIVE CENTRAL OFFICE
LONDON AND EASTERN REGION

32 SMITH SQUARE, WESTMINSTER, LONDON SW1P 3HH
TEL: 0171-222 9000 FAX: 0171-222 1135

24 NEWMARKET ROAD, CAMBRIDGE CB5 8DT
TEL: 01223 355281 FAX: 01223 323381
LONDON

Please reply to:

Mr Harry Tartt
26 Baildon Street,
Deptford,
LONDON SE8 4BQ

17th June 1996

Dear Mr Tartt,

BRITISH BEEF

Thank you for your letter detailing what you and your friends have been doing to support the campaign for British Beef. This is most encouraging and I am delighted to hear that you have had a good response.

Turning to the specific question you raise, whilst I am not an expert I do know from my days in Agriculture that Gelatine, Tallow and Semen are not involved in hamburgers and in the case of the Semen this relates to breeding and would not be anywhere near the food chain.

I trust this is of some use to you.

Yours sincerely

TIM R COWELL OBE
Regional Director

TC/sjo/june17.let11
Regional Director: TIM R COWELL OBE
Deputy Regional Director: GARETH J FOX
Campaign Executives: PAUL BURRETT MA, HUGH O'BRIEN

CONSERVATIVE

26 Baildon Street

Deptford

London SE8 4BQ.

Conservative Fmily Campaign

24 Marmona Road

London SE22 ORX.

Dear Hugh McKinney,

As an old man I have a lot of concerns regarding the education of the youngsters. Just down the road from me lives a young lad called Kenny Pringle and he is a real handful! Now, this lad is FOURTEEN YEARS OLD AND DRIVES HIS DAD'S CAR TO SCHOOL!! Not only that, but he parks it right next to the headmasters car! Good God, behaviour like that would've been unthikable in my day.

But you see, we had corporal punishment then. I remember one teacher, Mr. Tebbit, who actually punched children in the face if they misbehaved. He did it to me once for sneezing in assembly – I didn't do it again rest assured! I tell you what though, he had the most well-Behaved class in the school! It makes me chuckle to remember how my nose swelled up! On a more serious note, Can't we bring back corporal punishemnt to stop yobbish behaviour? Can we eliminate the Kenny Pringles of this world? Is it the break-down of the family to blame? What will the Conservatives do about it?

Harold Tartt. (A concerned pensioner)

CONSERVATIVE FAMILY CAMPAIGN

Bringing the family back into focus

15 Anthony Wall, Warfield, Berks RG42 3UL.

Chairman: Hugh McKinney MA
Tel: 01344 483 820

Vice Chairman: Guy Hordern MA JP
Tel: 0121 440 1738

President: Julian Brazier MA TD MP

24th June, 1996

Harold Tartt,
26, Baildon Street,
London,
SE8 4BQ

Dear Mr. Tartt,

Thank you for your recent letter. I totally agree with the concerns you have expressed.

I also agree with the means you have suggested of dealing with the Kenny Pringles of this world and Conservative Family Campaign takes a very robust line on corporal punishment.

When I proposed the Law and Order motion at the Conservative Party Conference two years ago I publicly called for its re-introduction and the support I received from those present and those outside was staggering.

I regret that the left-wing, liberal attitudes of the 1960s epitomised by Roy Jenkins and Quentin Hogg and perpetuated through the broadcasting media has created a situation where more young people feel they can challenge authority and this has damaged the notion of respect perhaps irrevocably.

However, we shall not give up. Decent, well-mannered people are still in the majority in this country, and we will continue to call for, initiate and support such measures as corporal punishment and effective means of control on parents and recalcitrant children.

Thank you for taking the time and trouble to write.

Yours sincerely,

Hugh McKinney,
Chairman

26 Baildon Street

Deptford

London SE8 4BQ.

Dear Mark Fowler,

First off, I'm sorry about your dad dying - it's understandable you're upSet. We all are. But what I want to say is - I know how you feel - recentley Bones, my dog and long-time friend and companion died. Since he has been gone I have felt very lonely, but I'll always have the memory of him. I still ocassionaly see him in my mind's eye though, whether he's asleep in the corner, chewing his plastic bone or licking himself in front of the t.v. What Im trying to say is, Arthur'll still be with you, even if he is dead.

Could you reply to my letter this time? Maybe send a photo of yourself (smiling eh?)

Keep your chin up mate.

Harold Tartt.

TODD CARTY

26 Baildon Street
Deptford
London SE8 4BQ.

William Hill Customer Relations
Greenside House,
50 STation Road,
Wood Green,
London N22 4TP.

Dear paul Roffe,

Could you tell me what would be the odds on me winning the the jackpot on the National Lottery?

Could I lay a bet on me to win?

I await YOur reply.

Customer Relations Department
Helpline 0990 181715
Greenside House, 50 Station Road, Wood Green, London N22 4TP.

DS/AN

2nd July 1996

Mr H. Tartt,
26, Baildon Street,
Deptford,
London,
SE8 4DQ.

Dear Mr Tartt,

Thank you for your letter received 29th June 1996.

The odds about any £1.00 line winning the Jackpot on the National Lottery are approximately 14 million to 1. Regrettably, legally, we are unable to offer odds on the possibility of your success.

Yours sincerely,

London se8 4BQ.

Dear Dame Barbara Cartland,

I think you're a wonderful woman m'lady (there really is 'nothing like a Dame'). I know that I'm just a poor old soul who can barely string a cohejent sentence together and therefore am worthy of your contempt - but, and I'm sure you don't care what I say, I am a huge fan.

I think you are a symbol of all that Englend once was; - decent, well mannered, well bought-up and well turned-out. In fact you are an institution. Unfortunately under this government they seem to close down and demolish all the old institutions - but they won't close you down Dame Barbara!

I won't expect a reply M'lady, though living alone in my flat, recieving letters is my only sauce of pleasure.

Yours admiringly,

Harold Tartt.

From: Dame Barbara Cartland, D.B.E. D.St.J.

19th July 1996

Dear Mr. Tartt

Thank you so much for your letter. It was very kind of you to write to me and I do agree with the things you say.

Things are certainly not what they used to be, but it is people like you and me who must fight for better times and to bring back the old standards.

Thank you again for taking the time to write to me. With all my best wishes,

26 Baildon Street
Deptford
London Se8 4BQ..

Dear Dame Barbara Cartland,

I'm glad that you agreed with me about the declining moral
standards of this once great country of ours. I fought a war
for this country and was injured.

I greatly admire you and though I don't read your books (i'm
a man) I think you look splendid for your age. Which is what
I want to talk to you about. You see, my pal, Billy Baxter
reckons that you are 105 years old! That's not true is it?

Could you let me know?
And if you are, tell me how you do it!!

Yours in deference,

Harold Tartt.

DAME BARBARA CARTLAND'S magical new Vitamins not only save time and trouble but also ensure that the taker remains young in body and brain.

SAFEGUARD. This one small tablet contains five different Vitamins and Minerals which make those who take it remain, for longer, much younger and more beautiful. These are Vitamins E, C and Beta Carotene, and Minerals Zinc and Selenium.
Cost for one month's supply is £8.95p.

EASY LIFE. One small tablet of this contains nine essential Vitamins and Minerals to keep you young and active for years.
Among the ingredients are the B. Vitamins, and Vitamin C plus the Biofl_____ds and Vitamin E.

BARBARA CARTLAND'S CHOICE ___
EASYLIFE will be availabl___
one month's supply exclus___
Ltd, Castle Ashby, North___

'I REACH FOR THE STARS' IS THE 6___
BOOK I HAVE WRITTEN AND I DO WAN___
TO READ IT. I AM STILL WRITING___
BOOK EVERY TWO WEEKS. THE 600T___
COSTS £14.95 AND IF YOU CANNOT___
AT YOUR LOCAL BOOK SHOP, PLEAS___
TO THE PUBLISHERS, ROBSON BOO___
BOLSOVER HOUSE. 5 - 6 CLIPSTO___
LONDON. W1P 7EB. ENCLOSING P___
PACKING

Barbara Cartland

Author of over 600 books
650 MILLION SOLD OVER THE WORLD

26 Baildon STreet

Deptford

London SE8 4BQ.

Dear Queen Mother,

God bless you ma'am.

I'm writing to you because quite frankly there's no one else like you around no more (except maybe Barbara Cartland, but I think she's lost it now). I think the way you got over your hip operation was marvelous (mind you, you didn't have the NHS to contend with - I've been waiting for an appointment to have my piles sorted for six months!). Any way, I've written you a poem:

During the war when Buck House was hit
The folks in the East End was all upset
But you visited them and looked them all in the eye
'Now I know how you feel' then you said goodbye.
And as the 'Enders watched your gold coach disappear,
they said, 'You're one of us Ma'am' and all shed a tear.

God bless.

Harry Tartt.

P.S. Could I have a signed photo?

CLARENCE HOUSE
S.W. I

1st July 1996

Dear Mr. Tartt,

Queen Elizabeth The Queen Mother has asked me to thank you for your letter, and the poem you sent to Her Majesty.

The Queen Mother appreciated all your kind remarks, but Her Majesty regrets that it is not possible to grant your wish. The reason is that members of the Royal Family receive so many requests for photographs and autographs that a strict rule has had to be made that these are only given to personal friends or for official purposes.

I am sorry to send you this reply, which may cause disappointment, but I am to convey to you an expression of The Queen Mother's very best wishes.

Yours sincerely,

Jane Walker Okeover.

Lady-in-Waiting

Mr. H. Tartt.

26 Baildon Street

Deptford

London SE8 4BQ.

Dear Teresa Gorman M.P.

We have started a 'Backing British Beef' campaign at my regular
pub - The Angry Toad - would you send us a photo of your good
self with a suitable inscription? I believe Mad Cow Desease is
greatly exagerated but we need the likes of you to make that
official!

I've been eating Beef for donkeys years now and I'm still unable
to lick my eyeball, and the only time *my* knees buckle is when
I've drunk too much beer!!

Awaiting Your reply,

TERESA GORMAN, M.P. FOR BILLERICAY

Constituency includes Billericay, Burstead, Bulphan, Corringham, Fobbing, Homesteads, Horndon-on-the-Hill,
Laindon, Orsett, Ramsden Bellhouse, Stanford-le-Hope, Wickford.
Surgeries every third Saturday. Tel: 071-219 5171 or write to House of Commons, London SW1A 0AA.

To Harold Tarft

Best wishes in your

Campaign to Back

British Beef

Teresa

Har

Printed by Fidelity Colour (0208) 544066

26 Baildon Street

Deptford

London SE8 4BQ.

Dear John Birt (Director General B.B.C),

Seeing as you've just lost the Queen's Christmas Broadcast along
with most of the football, cricket and rugby - why exactly do i
have to paya licence fee? To watch the rubbish the B.B.C puts
out? I tell you something, whenever I switch to your chanel
there's either some berk dressed as a copper screaming, 'Go, go
go!' or there's a bloody documentary following some poor little
kid about to have his leg chopped off! Is that what we pay for?
Or is it for The All-New Liver Birds? Is it? And do we pay for
two lager louts to sit on a sofa, talk about footie and scratch
their heads whenever they say something smart? Or, as I expect,
do we pay for Emma Thompson to prance around some crumbling
estate dressed in period costume?

Besides, I don't even watch B.B.C. no more, so doeS that make me
exempt from paying the licence fee? Does it?

Yours

Harry Tartt.

2 August 1996

Mr H Tartt
26 Baildon Street
Deptford
London
SE8 4BQ

BRITISH BROADCASTING CORPORATION
VILLIERS HOUSE
THE BROADWAY
EALING
LONDON W5 2PA
TELEPHONE: 0181-743 8000

Dear Mr Tartt

Thank you for your recent letter, addressed to the Director-General. I have been asked to reply.

I think the first point I should make is that the BBC does provide a considerable service in exchange for the licence fee. For £89.50 a year, or 25p a day, we supply two television channels, five radio networks and a full range of regional and local broadcasting. Recent research has suggested that the average licence-holding household watches or listens to about 36 hours of BBC programmes each week, at an hourly cost of about 5p. We like to think that this represents good value for money. Incidentally, we do all this on an income that is less than the cost of the single ITV channel.

I am sorry that you are having difficulty in finding programmes which you enjoy, but it is unavoidable that, with an audience of so many millions, we cannot possibly cater for all tastes at all times, and enjoyment is a very personal matter. I can assure you that we do strive to provide programmes for everyone, and I hope that, if you look across the whole range of the BBC's output, you will find something soon to suit your taste.

Yours sincerely

Sue McCoulough
Viewer & Listener Correspondence

26 Baildon Street
Deptford
London SE8 4BQ.

Conservative and Unionist Central Office
32 Smith Square
London SW1.

Dear Sir or Miss,

I have to say I have not been greatly impressed with your posters
depicting Tony Blair as Satan - I find them scary and nasty.
Don't get me wrong, I don't trusT the Labour as far as I can spit
them - I remember the Winter Of Discomfort only too well. I just
think a poster rethink could be in order. If you're interested, I
have a few suggestions vis a vis the election campain;

How about a giant picture of of Tony Blair, John Prescott and
Gordon Browne all dressed in baby bonnetts above the heading,
'Labour Pains'? Could work, eh?

Or maybe the slogan 'Better The Devil You Know - vote
Conservative.' Seeing as that's what most people in Britain said
last time round, might ring a bell!

I have lots more ideas if you'd care to let me know what you
think of these.

Yours in faith,

Harold Tartt.

P.S. Perhaps a good way of ensuring election success would be to
reply to people who have taken the trouble to write to you.

CONSERVATIVE

19 September 1996

Mr Harold Tartt
26 Baildon Street
Deptford
London
SE8 4BQ

Dear Mr. Tartt,

The Party Chairman has asked me to thank you for your recent letter to him.

Thank you for taking the time to write, and share your comments and suggestions with us, in regard to the presentation of Conservative Party policies and our media campaign.

Although our media campaign is prepared in-house, we appreciated your sharing your ideas with us. Please be assured that your comments and ideas have been noted, and will be brought to the attention of our policy unit.

With all our good wishes to you.

Yours sincerely,

N. MORGAN (MRS)
Public Correspondence

26 Baildon Street
Deptford
London SE8 4BQ.

Dear Lionel Blair,

I am a huge fan of you - you realy are a wonderful dancer - truley top-class.
I also think that you should feel honoured to have a peice of cockney-ryhming slang
named after you (Lionel Blairs = flairs). Not many people are given that honour in
their life-time, the only other one I can think of is dear old Eartha Kitt (though I dont
think she'd be too chuffed to hear what *her* name translates to!).
Anyhow, could you send me an inscribed picture of yourself?

Thanks Lionel,

Harry Tartt. (Pensioner)

NO REPLY.

26 Baildon Street

DeptfOrd

London SE8 4BQ.

Dear William Hill Bookies,

Could you tell me is it possible to bet on how many horses will die in the next Grand National?

If it is can you give me some odds?

Much obliged,

Harry Tartt.

William HILL

Customer Relations Department
Helpline 0990 181715

Greenside House, 50 Station Road, Wood Green, London N22 4TP.

MB/AN

7th November 1996

Mr H. Tartt,
26, Baildon Street,
Deptford,
London,
SE8 4BQ.

Dear Mr Tartt,

Thank you for your recent letter.

Regrettably we are unable to offer you the odds you have requested as we would not wish to quote on an eventuality that may be considered by some sections of the public to be in bad taste.

Nevertheless we thank you for taking the trouble to write.

Yours sincerely,

Michael Bateman
<u>Customer Relations Department</u>

William Hill Organization Limited. Registered Office: Greenside House, 50 Station Road, Wood Green, London N22 4TP. Reg. No. 278208 England

26 Baildon Street
Deptford
London SE8 4BQ.

Dear Sam Hamman (Director of Wimbledon Football Club),

I recentley frequented an up-market eating establishment with a lady aquiantance of mine (the Widow Johnson). We were having a lovely time up until a group of rowdies upset us both - I'm sorry to say it turned out that apparently some of them were footballers at your club!

It started off with them laughing at my large bottle of brown sauce. Now, I can understand them finding this unusual in an Indian restaurant but I think that's my business - anyhow, I let them have their fun but soon they started to get rude. A couple of them kept sniffing in my direction and blowing raspberries - now I know for certain I didn't drop any in there, and I had a bath before I went out but all this toilet humour put the Widow Johnson off her pudding and we left in a hurry.

Now, is this anyway for professional footie players to behave? Would the old-time greats have conducted themselves like this? Would the late Tommy Lawton have behaved in this manner? Or Nat Lofthouse? Or the late, great 'Jumpin'' Kenny Calhoun? I don't think so.

I'd like an apology for me and the Widow Johnson.

Yours in hope,

Harry Tartt.

Wimbledon Football Club Ltd

Selhurst Park Stadium London SE25 6PY Telephone 0181-771 2233 Fax 0181-768 0640

Mr Harry Tartt
26 Baildon Street
Deptford
London SE8 4BQ

20 November 1996

Dear Mr Tartt,

Mr Hammam has seen your letter and would like to get to the bottom of this. We have tried to 'phone you but your number is not listed.

It is totally unacceptable for anyone to behave in the manner described in your letter and we would therefore apologise to you and Mrs Johnson for any inconvenience that has arisen.

Even though it does not redress the situation, we would be glad if you and Mrs Johnson would accept our invitation to any of our Home games. We attach, for your convenience, our fixture list. Please contact me to arrange matters on your behalf, if you so wish.

Yours sincerely,

Stephanie Wilkes

Stephanie Wilkes
Secretary to Mr Sam Hammam

Enc

SPONSORED BY **ELONEX**

PERSONAL CO

VAT No. 561 8923 18   Registered in England No. 811820   Registered Office Selhur

FIXTURES
96/97
WIMBLEDON
FOOTBALL CLUB LTD

26 Baildon Street
Deptford
LONDON Se8 4BQ.

Dear Dutch Tourist Bored,

I am an elderley gent who thought in the war. Recentley I jumped at the chance to have a cheap weekend in Amsterdam (organised through The Legion). However having accidentley strayed from the rest of the crowd I found myself lost and walking down strange streets. It soon became dark and i began to get a little jittery. Somehow I found myself in the middle of the red Light District. I was shocked to see women displaying their wares in shop windows like so many sides of beef in a butcher shop. I was even approached by a dark chap who offered me drugs. I told him, 'you must be joking, a couple of Benalin and I'm out for the count!' He began shouting at me and swearing nastily, I moved on as a group of his mates started surrounding me and waving their arms around.

Naked women, prostitutes, pimps, it was terrifying - like a nightmare. After less than two hours I managed to leave the district and I fled as fast as my legs would carry me (one of them was injured in the war. The right one.)
Eventually I found my friends sitting outside a cafe. I exscused myself as I was feeling queer and went straight to my room to lay down. Now I'll get to why I'm writing to you - can you tell me why you don't have signposts and directions for the Red Light District? I say this so that people like me can avoid ending up there.

Although I had a terrible ordeal, I would like to return as I found the canals very nice.

I await your reply eagerley,

Harry Tartt.

Holland.
Netherlands Board of Tourism

PO Box 523
London SW1E 6NT
New Consumer Tel. No.:
0891 717 777 (premium charge)
Fax. No. 0171 828 7941
Tel Adv/PR 0171 828 7900 ext 281

Mr Harry Tartt
26 Baildon Street
Deptford
LONDON SE8 4BQ

ma
19 November 1996

Dear Mr Tartt,

Thank you for your letter informing us about your stay in Amsterdam. I very much regret your upsetting experience in the Red Light District.

I have passed your letter with your suggestion about sign posting the district to the Amsterdam Tourist Board.

I enclose a small Dutch token which I hope you will like and I very much hope your experience in Amsterdam will not prevent you from visiting our country again.

Yours sincerely,

Marielle Albers,
PR & Advertising Manager

cc: VVV Amsterdam
       NBT Amsterdam

26 Baildon Street
Deptford
London SE8 4BQ.

B.B.C Television Centre
Wood Lane
London W12 7RJ.

Dear Geoffrey Perkins,

I believe you'Re the fellow I should talk to. Now then, I want
to congratulate you on 6o years of programes. Well done. The
telly award program was good as well (though it did seem fixed).

I have had an idea for a new program for you too make - 'The
Return Of Porridge'!!! I know that Ronnie Barker's retired and
Richard beckinsale's dead, but after digging up the Liver Birds
and Reginald Perrin (minus Leonard Rossiter) I thought you might
as well do the best of the lot - it doesn't even have to be set
in a prison!

I think by using tried and trusted things rather than taking
comedy risks, you make the Licence Fee worthwhile - Besides,
these youngsters today couldn't write funny if you held a gun to
their heads. Incidentally, I've had a gun held to my head in the
war (I was injured in Palermo).

I hope you can take the trouble to write personally as I'm sure
you're very busy with something or other.

Yours,

Harry Tartt.

BRITISH BROADCASTING CORPORATION
TELEVISION CENTRE
WOOD LANE
LONDON W12 7RJ
TELEPHONE: 0181-743 8000

20 December 1996

Harry Tartt
26 Baildon Street
Deptford
London   SE8 4BQ

Dear Harry,

Thank you for your letter and your suggestion for resurrecting **"Porridge"**.
It's a trend we might also pursue with our current programmes. If Martin
Clunes and Neil Morrissey depart to that great theatre in the sky we could do
"Men Behaving Deadly", or when Richard Wilson goes we could produce
"Both Feet In The Grave".

Yours sincerely,

Paul Mayhew Archer
<u>Consultant, Comedy,</u>
<u>Entertainment, Television</u>

26 Baildon Street
deptford
London SE8 4BQ.

Dear Paul Mayhew Archer,

I detected from your reply to my Porridge-suggestion that you were laughing at me. This is sad. The last thing I need right now is for people to laugh at me, specially as my personal-plumbing's been shot to pieces ever since a tennis-related incident dating back to 1965.

I think the licence-fee's a joke and the B.B.C should be privatised.

Yours sincerely,

Harry Tartt.

P.S. were you responsible for Two By Four Children?

NO REPLY.

26 Baildon Street

DEptford

London SE8 4BQ.

Stonewall Lobby Group,

Dear Sir,

I was given your adress by a musician called Andre (he plays keyboard at The Angry Toad of a sunday - he's quite good actually, and not a bad fellow!). Anyway, the point is, during the summer I was up West buying myself some specialised pants, upon coming out of the shop with every intention of heading for the nearest cafe, I found myseLf surrounded by thousands of (mainly) men blowing whistles (which played hell with my tinitus). Before I knew it my cloth cap was removed and replaced with a big floppy sun-hat. It soon became apparent (judging by some of the lewd remarks made to me) that I was in the middle of a Gay Rights march (which I've got nothing against). Before I could make my escape I was hoisted onto a type of float and made to dance with a drag queen.

I have to say I think I'm open-Minded but the way that 'woman' ground 'her' body against me (to everyones great delight) was obsene. I felt ashamed. I still get upset when I think about it. Can you explain what all this was about?

And was a cap handed in?

I await a reply,

Harry Tartt.

Stonewall
Working for lesbian and gay equality

16 Clerkenwell Close
London EC1R 0AA
Telephone: 0171 336 8860
Facsimile: 0171 336 8864

Harry Tartt
26 Baildon Street
Deptford
London
SE8 4BQ
14th January 1997

Ref: IND/TARTT/140197/PJ

Dear Mr Tartt,

'Gay Pride' march.

Thank you for your letter.

I imagine that the event which you encountered was the annual 'Gay Pride' march.

The organisers of this event can be contacted at the following address:

The Pride Trust
Suite 28
Eurolink Centre
49 Effra Rd
London
SW2 1BZ

I hope that this is helpful.

Yours sincerely,

Philip Jones
Administrator

The Stonewall Group Limited Company
Registration Number: 02412299

26 Baildon STreet
Deptford
London SE8 4BQ.

Dear Manager Prince Of Wales Theatre,

Back in the fifties I took a lady-friend along to your theatre to
see a show featuring a young Kenny Calhoun. At great expense I
shelled out for one of the boxes. At the end of the show I
clapped and cheered so enthusiastically, I fell out of the box
and into the orchestra-pit. Luckily the only thing damaged was a
french horn and a timpani drum. Do you have a record of this
incident as no-one believes me?

I await your reply,

Harry Tartt.

PRINCE OF WALES THEATRE

(Controlled by Delfont Mackintosh Theatres Ltd.)

31 COVENTRY STREET : LONDON : W1V 8AS

GENERAL MANAGER . MIKE CHURCHILL

Telephone : 0171 930 1867
Facsimile : 0171 930 5108

Harry Tartt
26 Baildon Street
Deptford
London
SE8 4BQ

9th. January 1997

Dear Mr Tartt,

I thank you for your letter which caused me much amusement.

I regret, however, that you are probably confusing this theatre with another as Kenny Calhoun has not appeared at this theatre. In addition, if you were to fall out of one of our two boxes, you would not fall into the pit but into the stalls some 15ft. below and undoubtedly hurt yourself!

For your information, I am enclosing a list of the shows staged here since the building opened so that you can see the artist did not appear here.

I do hope that you track down the theatre where you had your adventure.

Yours sincerely,

M.Churchill

The Prince of Wales Theatre Ltd
Registered in England No 2522736
Registered Office 7 Soho Street, London W1V 5FA

26 Baildon Street
Deptford
London SE8 4BQ.

Claire Evans,(Poetry Today)

THE FIVE WEEK WAR

When Barry Carr was called up during the Second World War,
he left a family both hungry and poor
He wanted to go where the bullets danced,
A means of escape, a brand new chance!

But five weeks later and stripped to his pants
he staggered across the fields of Palermo.
Drunk on excitement and local vino,
Barry tripped over a tent peg and smashed his ankle,
before getting it crushed by a jeep and a Colonel.

A couple of weeks, dressed only in nightie,
He was told by a doctor, 'we're sending you back to Old
Blighty!'

Now, fifty-five years later and Barry's fine,
but from time to time it plays on his mind,
For Barry Carr the Second World War
Will always be remembered as The Five Week War.

I hope you like it, it's very personal.

Yours sincerely,

Harry Tartt.

P.S. How much will you pay me if it's published?

The Five Week War

When Barry Carr was called up during the Second World War,
he left a family both hungry and poor
He wanted to go where the bullets danced,
A means of escape, a brand new chance!

But five weeks later and stripped to his pants
he staggered across the fields of Palermo.
Drunk on excitement and local vino,
Barry tripped over a tent peg and smashed his ankle,
before getting it crushed by a jeep and a Colonel.

A couple of weeks, dressed only in nightie,
He was told by a doctor, 'We're sending you back to Old Blighty!'

Now, fifty-five years later and Barry's fine,
but from time to time it plays on his mind,
For Barry Carr the Second World War
Will always be remembered as *The Five Week War*.

Harry Tartt

PROOF
PLEASE CHECKMARK ERRORS
FOR CORRECTION, SIGN AND
RETURN BY THE DEADLINE

SIGNATURE:.................................

Upper Dee Mill,
Llangollen LL20 8SD

poetry Pt today

Telephone : 01978 869109
Fax : 01978 869110

Dear Harry, Thank you for submitting 'The Five Week War'. I
have put it to the editors for consideration for our next
anthology. At the moment we do not pay royalties for
work - when we are in a profit situation we will look at
it again! If you are interested in getting paid for your
work try sending into magazines, they are often in receipt
of grants and will pay small amounts for work.
regards Kelly Olsen

Poetry Today is an imprint of β Penhaligon Page LIMITED

Mr H Tartt
26 Baildon Street
Deptford
London
SE8 4BQ

15 January 1997

Dear Harry

I am writing with reference to the poetry you have submitted to Poetry Today. As you know we are working on a new project that will bring together good, contemporary and traditional poetry in quality books. The aim is to build a solid library of books that represent the poets and poetry of the time.

From The Heart will be the fifth book of this library and we have carefully selected around three hundred poems for this title, including your poem *The Five Week War*.

Every book has its own character and *From The Heart* will contain poetry of contemporary style, both rhyming and non-rhyming, which is well written and accessible. The book will run to about three hundred pages, in a format large enough to contain both poem and notes about the poet and/or poem (Poet's Notes) on each page. *From The Heart* will be hard bound using traditional methods and high quality materials.

Whilst ensuring good quality we have tried to keep the price of *From The Heart* within reach of as wide an audience as possible, the retail price of £26.95 is, I feel, excellent value for money. We do ask contributors to purchase at least one copy of the book at a reduced price of £21.50. Unfortunately poetry is a notoriously difficult market (most new poetry is published with subsidies) and whilst we are hoping to build both good reputation and sales, we must ensure initial costs are met. The nature of printing means the more books that are printed in one run, the lower in price each book becomes, therefore, once you have purchased one copy of *From The Heart*, further copies will cost only £15.00. This price is only available to contributors.

Poetry Today is an imprint of **β Penhaligon Page** LIMITED

The
copie.

Publi:
explai.
questi(

I look

Yours sincerely

Julie Bomber

26 Baildon STreet

Deptford

London SE8 4BQ.

Football Association

16 Lancaster Gate

London W2.

Dear Graham Kelly,

I am an old man, on a pension, who can't afford the Football no more. but, i will be watching the European Championships on television. Now then, having little money, I would like to get behind our lads - so, could you send me a flag to show from my window? It'd be a grand gesture on your part and it'd cheer me up no end.

My dad was actually at the famous Wembley White Horse Final, one of two hundred thousand people!! And he always swore that the famous white horse peed on his shoe - but you could never tell with my dad - he was a great story-teller!

Look forward to receiving your package,

Harry Tart

26 Baildon Street

Deptford

London SE8 4BQ.

Dear Terry Wogan,

Hello. Top o' the morning to you! Seriously though, I just wanted to say thet your breezy charm
first thing of a morning always sets me up for the day ahead (no matter how blooming awful it
turns out to be) and more often than not you make me chuckle over my porridge.

I'm glad that you're back on radio as I believe you are at your most comfortable being unseen – I'm
not saying your t.v career didn'T work – just that maybe radio is your real home, know what I
mean? But PLEASE carry on hosting the European Song Contest, cause that always makes me
chuckle. My God, some of those foreign songs eh? – 'Bang a Bang a Catermaran' – Good heavens!!

Any road up, could you send me a photo of you with an inscription purtaining to The said European
Song Contest?

Much obliged,

Harry Tartt.

26 Baildon Street
Deptford
London SE8 4BQ.

Customer Realations
Wimpy International Ltd,
The Listons,
Liston Road, Marlow,
Bucks.

Dear Sir or Miss,

I have read that due to the beef crisis your custom has been greatly affected. I want to say that as far as I'm concerned - it's all nonsense, I'll be eating the stuff till the cows come home. No, what I want to say is if you want to claw back some custom how about a little gesture? Something to show good faith. A good start would be to stop charging ten pence for a silly little sachet of ketchup.

Awaiting your repLy,

Harry Tartt.

NO REPLY

To HARRY —
LGE2 fond memories of
the good old bad days!
All the best. Derek Jameson **DEREK JAMESON**

B.B.C. Radio and He
Broadcasting House
Portland Place
London W.1

Dear Derek Jameson,

Mawnin'! Stand by yer beds! Tartt here!

Seriously, I'm just writing to tell you how much I used to enjoy
your show of a morning - that is, up until last week when my
wireless dropped in the fish tank! (eletrocuted me bloody Carp an
all!)

Still, life goes on and I suspect that rather like me, you reckon
the old days was best - I'M sure they were! God, the laughs we
had eh? But times weren't always easy - I was injured in Palermo
during the war you know!

Could you send me a photo of your good self with an inscription
perhaps purtaining to the Good Old Days?

Good on you mate,

Harry Tartt.

26 Baildon Street
Deptford
LondoN Se8 4BQ.

Dear Producers of the Kilroy Show,

I am an elderley gent and for the past few years have been gently stepping out with a woman named Johnson. Now, a few months back she took it upon herself to visit the Kilroy Show which was all about being elderley and having sexual relations. Now, not being active in that department (due to a bowling accident in 1968) I decided not to attend, and watched it on the telly. Kilroy as usual spent the whole show preening himself and swanning about, but what really got my goat was the way he got so familiar with the women audience members, touching their knees and all that, in his flirty way. When Mrs. Johnson made a point he perched himself by her (their knees pressed tight together) and laid on his smarm with a trowel. She started coming on like a love-sick schoolgirl (even though she's 78 in August) , all giggly all doughey-eyed.

I must admit when I next saw her I got a bit aggrieved and showed her the rough end of my tongue. Things haven't been The same sinse. She never laughs at my jokes and is always comparing me to The Golden Boy.

In short, Kilroy has driven a wedge between us with his silver tongue and ready charm. Doesn't he as a t.v. personality, have a responsibility not to wreck peoples lives? Can his flirting be controlled? Perhaps a fine system could be impimented.

I'd appreciate a reply as I pay a licence fee for some reason.

Harry Tartt Esq.

NO REPLY.

26 BaildOn Street

deptford

London Se8 4BQ.

Dear National Peanut Council of America,

A few years ago a good friends grandchild stuck a peanut in my ear. Ever since I have suffered greatly with my hearing. Is it there fore possible for you to make a contribution towards me obtaining hearing aid? The only facts I can give you are ; the incident happened in July 1987, and the peanut was a salted Percy Dalton.

please write back as I need to get this hearing aid urgent.

Yours in hope,

Harry Tartt. (war veteran)

NO REPLY.

26 Baildon Street
Deptford
London SE8 4BQ.

Dear Zelda West Meads (You Magazine),

I am a man of advancing years who's only partner for the past seventeen was an flea-bitten old mutt called Bones. Bones died a few months back and I have beena lonely man since. However, lately I had the good fortune to meet up after many years with The Widow Johnson - I knew her back when she wasn't even married, let alone widowed! (She used to gut chickens with my cousin). Anyhow, I suppose you could say I've been stepping out with her lately.

This is all well and fine, but on the last couple of dates she has alluded to having 'relations' with me. I was shocked (I missed out on a full-house during the bingo!) Now, being in my seventh decade and having a gammy leg (war injury) I don't know if I can still do it! Am I up to it? What if I fail? Or pull something?

How can I approach this delicate situation?

Please reply quickly as I don't know if I can fend her off for much longer!

Yours anxiously,

Harry Tartt.

Dear Harry Tartt

Thank you very much for writing to me. I do try to answer as many letters as possible. But due to the number of letters I receive it will take a few weeks before I can reply. So I have also enclosed the names and telephone numbers of several organisations, some of which you may find helpful.

For marital and relationship problems, contact your nearest branch of Relate, the marriage guidance organisation. They offer a confidential counselling service. Phone numbers are listed in the directory.

Depending on your religion, there is also the Catholic Marriage Advisory Council, H.Q. No: 0171-371 1341.

The Jewish Marriage Council is only available in London and Manchester. London phone number: 0181-203 6311. Manchester phone number: 0161-740 5764. Crisis line for London area: 0181-203 6211. Outside London crisis line: 0345-581999. charged at local rate.

The Samaritans, who offer an excellent 24-hour telephone service, provide confidential emotional support for people in crisis. Phone numbers in local directories.

Bereavement counselling is available from Cruse's telephone line, open Monday to Friday, 9.30am to 5pm, on 0181-332 7227.

Remember also you can consult your family doctor if you are suffering from depression or need to talk through your problems so that she or he too can refer you to whatever is available in your area.

I do hope you find this helpful.

Yours sincerely

Zelda West-Meads

Zelda West-Meads

Northcliffe House, 2 Derry Street, Kensington, London W8 5TT
Telephone: 0171-938 6000
Editorial Dept. Fax: 0171-938 1488 Fashion Dept. Fax: 0171-938 6272
A division of Associated Newspapers Limited
Reg. No: 84121 ENGLAND

26 Baildon Street

Deptford

London SE8 4Bq.

Manager London Palladium,

Dear sir or Miss,

I wonder if you can help me, you see, I'm trying to find any information on my theatrical family and in particular Uncle George. George was a music-hall favorite and leader of the troupe known as 'The Tumbling Tartts'. the exact nature of their act is unclear, but it was said to involve a lot of tumbling.

Before my father passed off, he told me that the Tumbling Tartts' crowning moment of glory was when they performed at the Palladium. The details are sketchy but I believe it was 1907 and they were part of a variety night that ended with an incident involving them and some clowns.

If you have any information regarding The Tumbling Tartts and the supposedly notorious night I would be very grateful.

Yours awaiting a reply,

Harry Tartt.

LONDON PALLADIUM

ARGYLL STREET, LONDON W1A 3AB.   TELEPHONE (0171) 437 6678.   STAGE DOOR (0171) 437 1278.
BOX OFFICE (0171) 494 5020

January 31st 1997

H. Tartt, Esq.,
26, Baildon Street,
Deptford,
London. SE8 4BQ.

Dear Mr. Tartt,

I am in receipt of your letter requesting information

regarding your Uncle and the act known as 'The Tumbling

Tartts' and regret that I am unable to help you, we have no

record of this hatsoever.

Yours faithfully,
For Stoll Moss Theatres Limited

Brenda Murray.

Advertising Manager.

STOLL MOSS THEATRES LIMITED, A MEMBER OF THE HEYTESBURY GROUP
REGISTERED OFFICE: MANOR HOUSE, 21 SOHO SQUARE, LONDON W1V 5FD
REGISTERED IN ENGLAND Nº 233200

26 Baildon Street
Deptford
London SE8 4BQ.

Police Complaints Authority
10 Great George Street
London SW1.

Dear Officer,

Having recentley ended up in someone's garden hedge as a result of a speeding police car, I have (reluctantly)taken the unusual step of putting my opinions in print, (so to speak). Whilst I fully appreciate that "Z-Cars" was a fabulous program, I do beleive we need more bobby's on the beat. The reign of terror recentley inflicted on my local community by one Kenny Pringle, I beleive, could have been avoided by a local copper administering the occasional, and strategic clip round the bonce. Good heavens, in my day a copper wasnt afraid to kick you in the rear if you had done wrong. As a child I remember a P.C. Potter who actualy swung me round by my ears for harrassing the Sally Army. I never complained. In fact, years later I actually thanked him. Come to think of it, I ended up in a hedge that day as well. How times have changed!

Please, please, please listen to Joe Public - more bobbys on the beat!

Yours with respect but concern,

Mr. Harry Tartt. Pensioner.   NO REPLY

26 Baildon Street
Deptford
London SE8 4BQ.

Dear Zelad-West Meads,

I realise you are a very busy woman, but I've waited a couple of months for your reply, and I'm desperate. The Widow Johnson is still alluding to having 'relations', and with my tennis-related injury (groinal) I don't know if I'm up to the job (plus I'm seventy-two and have piles and a gammy leg).

Please reply quick, it's like she's on heat or something.

Yours urgently,

Harry Tartt.

you

THE MAIL ON SUNDAY

15th January 1997.

Dear Harry Tartt,

Thank you very much for your two letters. I was not sure if your first letter was entirely seriouse, but if it was I'm sorry I have not replied. I do get a lot of letters and it is sometimes difficult to answer them all but I do try.

I think a man has a right to say 'no' to the unwelcome advances of a woman, just as a woman also has the right to say 'no' to the unwanted attentions of a man. So if you do not want to get involved with ' the Widow Johnson 'I suggest you politely say no, tell her you think she is very nice but you are not interested in taking the relationship any further.

If on the other had you are quite attracted by the idea on a sexual relationship with her - being 72, with piles and a gammy leg should not be a hindrance. If you do have a problem getting or maintaining an erection with the help of an understanding and patient partner it will probably sort itself out. If not I suggest that you contact the Impotence Association help line on 0818 767 7791 for further help.

with kind regards

yours sincerely, *Zelda West-Meads*

Zelda West-Meads.

31

Northcliffe House, 2 Derry Street, Kensington, London W8 5TT
Telephone: 0171-938 6000
Editorial Dept. Fax: 0171-938 1488 Fashion Dept. Fax: 0171-938 6272
A division of Associated Newspapers Limited
Reg. No: 84121 ENGLAND

26 Baildon
Street
Deptford
London SE8 4BQ.

Dear Conservative Family Association,

I am very concerned about drugs. All around me I see abuse. Terrible. But what are the politicians doing about it? Nothing! It's infecting every part of society. I should know! Let me relate a story to you; -

Every year old folk such as myself are invited to The Deptford Creek Asian Community Centre for free food and some songs. This year (as you may have read in some of the lesser papers) there was a bit of an incident. During the course of the meal it soon became apparent that people was acting strangely (I'm not just talking about them that are senile), anyhow, before long it all got out of control and there was fist-fights and fornicating going on left, right and centre (I am embarressed to say I was involved in some scuffles). The police was called and my good friend (a normally law-abiding man called Billy) was carted away for knocking a policeman's hat off.

Anyway, once the broo-ha-ha had died down it was found out that someone had 'laced' the Beef Cobbler with magic mushrooms (drugs). I have a pretty good idea it was a young lad called Kenny Pringle, can't prove it, but he was serving the food and he keeps making jokes about it!

Now this was treated as a bit of a laugh by the papers, but some of us keep having 'flash-backs' (the police told us to expect these).

Surely all drugs must be banned? They're not even pleasant. What will the Conservatives do at the next election? I know a lot of old folk who are very concerned!

Yours,

Harry Tartt.

NO REPLY

26 Baildon Street

Deptford

London SE8 4BQ.

War Pensioners Welfare SErvice

218 Balham High Street.

London SW12 9Df.

Dear Mr Cattermole,

I have been thinking lately, during the war I was injured while serving in Palermo - the story being, after overdoing it on the local wine I tripped over a tent peg thus breaking my ankle. Sounds funny, wasn't.

Now, I wondered if it would be possible to claima war injury (it aches something awful in the winter) - if it is possible, perhaps it could be back-dated?

Please reply soon as I'M very old now and need the money.

Harry Tartt.   (pensioner)

Claim form WPA 1
From April 1995

War Pension - Claim Form

WAR PENSIONS AGENCY

This form is for making a first claim to War Pension if you served in His Majesty's or Her Majesty's (H M) Armed Forces. People who served in H M Armed Forces also include the Nursing and Auxiliary Services, the Ulster Defence Regiment who are now known as the Royal Irish Regiment, and the Home Guard.

You may be able to get a War Pension if you served

- during the 1914 - 18 War,

- at any time since 2 September 1939,

- in the Polish Forces under British Command during the 1939 - 45 War or in the Polish Resettlement Corps,

and you think your service

- caused you to suffer a wound, injury, disease or other condition. ✓

- made worse a disablement you had before or during service.

Part 1 About you

1. Please tell us about yourself

Surname	Tartt
Other names	HAROLD wellington
Any other ~~surname~~ nick-name you have had or are known as	"Flaky" *
Title	Mr / Mrs / Miss / Ms / Dr / Rev **mr.**

National Insurance number

Letters	Numbers					Letter
N						

Awarded for excellence

* "Flaky" was my nick-name in the Forces - not now.

26 Baildon Street

Deptford

London SE8 4BQ.

Dear Copyright Licensing Agency,

I have a friend and drinking companion by the name of Billy BAxter - now, he's about the only company I have since my dog Bones died - but lately he's been getting a bit on my wick. The reason being, he keeps stealing my jokes and stories. What's really annoying is when I tell them to him he never laughs (sometimes he yawns) yet on a couple of ocassions I've caught him telling the same stories to the regulars of The Angry Toad - and they all roar with laughter (Baxter included). On one ocassion I tried to tell them the story was mine and they thought I was being petty.

Now, would it be possible to copyright some of my stories that I haven't thusfar related to Billy Baxter? If so, how much would it cost me per story?

Yours awaiting a reply,

Harry Tartt.   NO REPLY

26 Baildon Street
Deptford
London
SE8 4BQ

Dear English Tourist Board,

I have come up with a completely fair way of earning money for this great country of ours. Following a recent visit to Wales I was disturbed to find out we had to pay <u>four pound twenty</u> to get in. To get into Wales!! This came as one hell of a shock as I'd just spent all my money on a slap-up breakfast at a Little Eater (Which as it goes cost a small fortune and tasted like rubber).

Now then, what I thought is - we're paying to get into Wales when alls they've got is The Royal Mint (which used to be ours), and Hadrian's Wall. Meanwhile we've got Buckingham Palace, The Tower Of London, Windsor Palace, The Houses of Parliment, The Queen, and countless other sites. Why don't we charge them double to come here? That'd be a whopping £8.40 per Welshman entering England - it'd rake in a fortune which could be used for increasing pensions for people like me who can't afford to visit the likes of Wales.

Let me know what youthink of the idea. I'm looking to get it copywrited so I can earn on it if it gets implimented.

Many Thanks and I await your reply,

Harry Tartt.

ENGLISH TOURIST BOARD

Thames Tower

Black's Road

London W6 9EL

England

Tel: 0181 846 9000

Fax: 0181 563 0302

Web: www.visitbritain.com

Direct Line: 0181 563 3394
Direct Fax: 0181 563 3350
RCarey@mail.bta.org.uk

ENGLISH
TOURIST BOARD

Mr. Harry Tartt
26 Baildon Street
Deptford
London SE8 4BQ

2 July 1999

Dear Mr. Tartt

Thank you for your wonderful letter which considerably brightened our day.

I fear that we cannot endorse your plan. Given that the English Tourist Board is charged with promoting tourism to England, we actually want all the Welshmen here that we can get. On the other hand, if we are lucky, our fellow countrymen will be deterred from travelling to this exotic destination and will spend their money here in England instead. All in all I can see that the present arrangements serve our purposes admirably.

However, far be it from us to deter an entrepreneur!

Yours sincerely,

Ros Carey
Head of Policy

PS. Why not go by train next time?

26 Baildon Street
Deptford
London SE8 4BQ.

Dear Nick rainsford M.P. and Head Of London Affairs,

I just wanted to tell you that The Millenial Celebrations look like they might be very enjoyable. This praise almost sticks in my throat as I was one of The Dome's biggest critics ("The Millenium Cone" I used to call it - it never caught on but it was funny enough at the time). I would also like to say that I beleive you would make a good Mayor for London - then again I'd vote for anyone rather than The Idiot Livingstone! His smarm campaign doesn't wash. In fact Ken Livingstone doesn't wash with me at all. I remember his GLC Loony Left shinanegans only too well. Fare's Fair? - Only if you was a black, bearded, womans libber, lesbian one parent family (and I dont want that to sound offensive, I'm not a racialist.) Still, I'll be candid with you - I'm backing Archer for Mayor(which is probabley what New Labour'll do if it means keeping Red Ken out!)

Anyhow, I'm getting on a bit and not only do I have a war wound, but I am also having some problems with my lady friend Mrs. Johnson - it's of a personal nature, her demands have left me quite raw and sensitive. So to cheer me up I'd love to visit the Dome - unfortunately on my pension I could never afford it. Would it be possible to send me a couple of free tickets? One for me and my lady friend? It would make my day it really would, and it might help to take the sour look off HER face - particularly if the Queen was there. Go on, it'd make a lovely story.

I'm looking forward to hearing fRom you (with some good news?)

Thanks Nick.
Harry Tartt. (War veteran and published poet).

HOUSE OF COMMONS

LONDON SW1A 0AA

Office 0171 219 5895
0171 219 2773
Fax   0171 219 2619

5 August 99

Dear Mr Tartt,

Thank you for your letter of 2 August.   I am sorry that you live just outside my constituency and therefore cannot take advantage of the Greenwich Card scheme available for residents of the London Borough of Greenwich.   There will be special concessions for pensioners and significant concessions for groups. It may well be worth your while going with a group of friends rather than just Mrs Johnson as this will further reduce the cost.   Attached is a sheet containing details of the costs.

I am afraid that I cannot provide you with free tickets as I am not being given any.

Thank you for your kind comments.

Yours sincerely,

Nick Raynsford MP

Mr H Tartt
26 Baildon Street
Deptford
London
SE8 4BQ

26 BAIldon Street

deptford

London SE8 4BQ.

Dear Jeffrey Archer,

I am just writing to you with a message of support from me and some of the locals of The Angry Toad Public House. Personally I hope you become mayor of London rather than Glenda Jackson, or the berk Livingstone. How ever, I believe that your campaign is delibarately being spiked by outsiders. Your innocent comments about blacks in the '50's has been hijacked by the right-on Brigade, and I for one am browned off with their form of dictatorship - it's all gone too far. Like you, I am not a racialist, but have recentley been on the receiving end of this tyrany myself. Not so long ago I attended the Welsh club in Surley with a pal of mine. Now, I was just having a bit of a laugh about the Welsh, when I was asked to leave and was then man- handled out of the place by a couple of gorillas (not actual gorillas, but they looked it). It was ridiculous, I didn't mean no offence, in fact some of my best friends are Welsh, particularly my old pal Taffy Edwards. But you see, this is where we are now - you can't say anything for fear of being asked to leave or being roughed up. Crazy, absolutely crazy.

Anyhow, what I want to say is we are all backing you for Mayor and could you send us a nice letter of support (to me, Andre and all the regulars at The Angry Toad). What we'd like is to get it framed and hung in the pub itself (we've already got Teresa Gorman and Willie Whitelaw hanging on the wall).

Could you also tell me how you'd sort out the public Transport.

God Bless,

Harry Tartt (war veteran and published pot)

Jeffrey Archer

House of Lords

Mr H Tartt
26 Baildon Street
Deptford
London SE8 4BQ

31st August 1999

Dear Mr Tartt,

Many thanks for your recent letter.

I have spent the past two and a half years researching the problems that Londoners face, and transport is my top priority. I thought you might like to see one of my recent papers that will give you a little background on my plans.

I do appreciate your taking the time to write, and am very grateful for your support, and that of Andre and all the regulars at *The Angry Toad*.

With best wishes

Yours sincerely

Jeffrey Archer

Action for London

ISSUE 2

JEFFREY ARCHER LOOKS AHEAD
— page 2

LABOUR'S ATTACK ON LONDON

abour is taking hundr...
unds a...

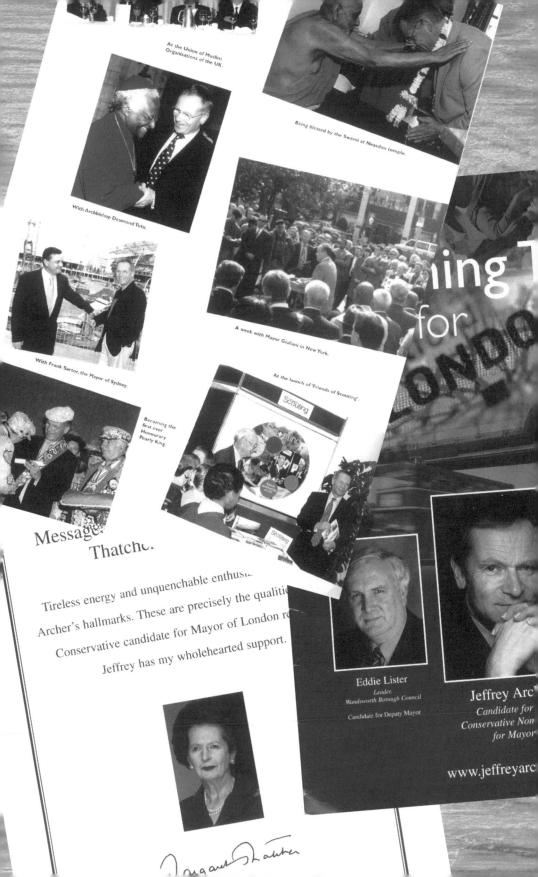

At the Union of Muslim Organisations of the UK.

Being blessed by the Swami at Neasden temple.

With Archbishop Desmond Tutu.

A week with Mayor Giuliani in New York.

With Frank Sartor, the Mayor of Sydney.

At the launch of 'Friends of Scouting'.

Becoming the first ever Honourary Pearly King.

Message
Thatcher

Tireless energy and unquenchable enthusi...
Archer's hallmarks. These are precisely the qualitie...
Conservative candidate for Mayor of London re...
Jeffrey has my wholehearted support.

Eddie Lister
Leader,
Wandsworth Borough Council

Candidate for Deputy Mayor

Jeffrey Arc
Candidate for
Conservative Non
for Mayor

www.jeffreyarc

26 Baildon Street

deptford

London SE8 4Bq.

Dear BBC Complaints Department,

The other night I accidentaly watched a program on your channel about Russian serial killers. Now, what I want to say is I dont realy pay my lisense fee in order to have the living daylights scared out of me. That same night, I must have been thrashing around in my sleep as the hatstand fell atop me. My screams sent the dog into a frenzy and he bit my ankle as I wrestled with what I thought was a killer (he also ripped up my cap). I dont mind telling you I was scared witless and stayed up the rest of the night watching Open University programs. I have been suffering ever sinse with my nerves (which were already shot to bits after having a gun pressed to my head during the war). Half of them Russian serial killers were barely out of short trousers for god sake!

If you must program horror, would it not be posible to put out a warning to old folk like myself who live alone?

yours,

Harry Tartt.

British Broadcasting Corporation PO Box 1116 Belfast BT2 7AJ Telephone 08700 100 222 Fax 01232 326453 E-Mail info@bbc.co.uk

BBC Information

Mr Harry Tartt
26 Baildon Street
Deptford
London
SE8 4BQ

Our Ref 1602167

31 August 1999

Dear Mr Tartt

Thank you for your recent letter regarding 'Inside Story – The Russian Cracker' on BBC ONE.
Please accept my apologies for the delay in replying.

I am very sorry that you were upset and distressed by this programme. Portraying violence presents continuing problems for broadcasters, and is the subject of very regular debate. The portrayal of violence on television is now subject to strict guidelines issued to all producers.

In general we believe there are circumstances in which the portrayal of violence is justified, but only for the credibility and integrity of the programme in question. We do not allow gratuitous scenes of violence, and from 9pm onwards, our television programmes are suitable only for adults. The BBC constantly monitors public attitudes as expressed by audience comments, research, correspondence and other sources of feedback, therefore your strong views on this subject have been sent to the programme makers for careful consideration.

Once again, thank you for taking the trouble to write to the BBC with your protest.

Yours sincerely

Clare Kenna
BBC Information

26 Baildon Street
Deptford
London Se8 4BQ.

Dear Edwin a Curry,

I have been following your career closely ever sinse the horrible mix up with your eggs. I really thought you was one to look out for, a real star (and a looker to boot!). So the other day when I saw your book in the library I leapt at it and read it there and then. Well, Edwina, you are a dark horse arent you? I dont mind telling you I got quite hot under the collar, it was steamy stuff indeed! The last time I read anything quite so close to the bone was when I stumbled upon dear old Cliff Michelmore's's Autobiography "A Life By The Docks".
Here's a short poem.

EDWINA

It began with eggs, then Northerners and gravy
Edwina, you are a controversial lady,
You spoke your mind, now you speak your heart
Your rampant passion all but did for this old Tartt.
As I dropped the Big Print book to the floor
And breathless, stumbled to the library door
"You left your cap" Shouted an assistant fair.
"Forget the cap, I need some air!"
I replied.

Could you send me a photo with a sexy message?

God bless you darling,

Harry tartt. Pensioner. Just.

Edwina Currie (signature)

LIVE

EDWINA CURRIE
CHASING MEN

ENJOYING LIFE LIKE
NEVER BEFORE ...

26 Baildon Street
Deptford
London SE8 4BQ.

Dear Customer Relations at British Airways,

I'm writing with regard to one of your recent adverts that has been on the telly. I have to say I find it strange that the best way you could think of to promote our country was to get a sneery yank to slag us off. My mate has told me that the yank is some famous journalist, and is famous for being outrageous - well he can be outrageous elsewhere - and not on my time!!!

In the advert, the yank sneers at all our funny customs. Well, I'll tell him one custom he forgot to mention - that of getting Foreigners to come on our screens and slag us off -then pay them for the privilidge. That's one of our queerest customs, definately.

Now, what I'm offering is MY services. I'm more than prepared to come on telly and list all the good things about this country, some of which I've listed below.

Queen Mother
The Millenium
Beefeaters
The Queen
A sense of humour
pubs
Football (the proper kind)
English breakfast.

And there's more where they come from.

Also, a good way of keeping your customers happy would be to reply to they're letters.

I hope you receive this in good health,

Harry Tartt. (Pensioner).

BRITISH AIRWAYS

02 September 1999

Mr H Tartt
26 Baildon Street
Deptford
London
SE8 4BQ

Our Ref: 000485085

Dear Mr Tartt

Thank you for writing to tell us about your disappointment with our latest advertisement on the television.

I am sorry that you have been dissatisfied with our advertising and marketing campaign to promote British Airways and assure you that your comments and suggestions have been noted and will be put forth in the next regular review.

British Airways prides itself on being a world leader in customer service and we are always disappointed if we have failed to meet the high standards our customers rightly expect from us. We welcome passenger comments whether positive or negative and I assure you we listen to what our customers have to say.

Thank you once again for writing in and we look forward to welcoming you on board one of our flights again soon.

Yours sincerely

Qaizalbash Sheikh
Customer Relations

Customer Relations

PO Box 10 (S506) Heathrow Airport London Hounslow Middlesex TW6 2JA United Kingdom
Tel 0345 222787 (UK Local Call Rate) + 44 (0) 20 8283 9500 Fax + 44 (0) 20 8759 4314

British Airways Plc Registered office: Waterside PO Box 365 Harmondsworth UB7 0GB Registered in England No. 1777777

BA13922

26 BAILDON STREET

DEPTFORD

LONDON SE8 4Bq

National Express.

Dear Sir or Miss,

Nowadays if I am traveling across Britain I only travel by coach, as it seems to be cheaper to fly to Constantinople than to use British Rail. There fore I have become quite familiar with the old National Express coaches. However, being of pensionable age and suffering from piles, a gammy leg, and problems with my plumbing - it is not always the most comfortable way to travel. This is not made easier by getting a coach driver who is determined to take "Rat-runs" across London, as did the driver I got recentley. Everytime I got comfortable (which is difficult with severe piles) he'd veer the coach sharply down some little bumpy streets. Now, he must have heard my howls of pain, but he continued like this for a good hour or so till we got out of London. By then, not only was I in agony, but I was damp as well (due to my medical condition).

When we got on a straight peice of road I managed to get down the front to have words with him. not only was he rude and un-sympethetic, but he kept calling me "grandad". He also seemed to be mocking me for the amusement of the other passengers. He said I should have bought my own rubber ring, and when I whispered about my plumbing problems, he said, and I quote: "why don't you stick your bum out the window to dry then?". I spent the rest of the journey sitting in a damp patch, in pain, feeling sorry for myself. What I want to know is - 1)Is this the state of travel in Britain as we enter the millenium? 2) Is this any way to treat an old war heroe? and 3) Will you even bother to respond, let alone apologise? The anwers, I reckon are: 1) yes. 2) No. and 3) probably not.

Yours in anger,

Harry Tartt.

NATIONAL EXPRESS »

TRAVEL £5 VOUCHER

FOR CONDITIONS SEE OVER

ISSUED BY
NATIONAL EXPRESS LTD., 4 VICARAGE ROAD, EDGBASTON, BIRMINGHAM B15 3ES

5NE 060381

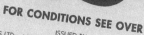

25 August 1999

Ref: M7124/78/1

Dear Mr Tartt

Thank you for your recent letter received at this office, from which I was sorry to learn of the problems you have outlined, and I would take this opportunity to ask you to accept our apologies.

In particular, I was most concerned to learn of the attitude of the driver which you encountered. All staff employed on our service should be as polite and helpful as possible and there is no excuse for the behaviour you describe.

You may rest assured that all the points which you have raised will be fully investigated and followed up in our endeavours to avoid any repetition, as customer comments are used as a basis to improve our standard of service.

In view of the circumstances and as a gesture of goodwill, I have pleasure in enclosing a Coach Travel Voucher to the value of £15.00, which I hope will go someway towards restoring your confidence in the service we provide.

May I take this opportunity to thank you for taking the trouble to contact us with your comments, as this provides us with invaluable feedback and enables appropriate corrective action to be taken.

Yours sincerely

Mandy Wray
Customer Relations Officer

NATIONAL EXPRESS LTD., REGISTERED IN ENGLAND NO. 232767
REGISTERED OFFICE: 4 VICARAGE ROAD, EDGBASTON, BIRMINGHAM B15 3ES.

26 Baildon Street
Deptford
London SE8 4BQ.

Dear Christian information,

To mis-quote my companion Mrs. Johnson I am "in a dark place and need to find a spirtual home". You see, following a horrific near-death expereince in Blackpool I have been through what she calls a "dark hour of the soul".

Now, she recomended that I send three questions to various religious groups in order to help me decide what faith I should be. Here are your questions -

My friend says there is no such thing as heaven but our heads just float about in space. Is that true?

My friend's grandson is a clever lad (even though he only wears black and never blinks), now in the pub the other night he suddenly announced that God is dead, which came as a bit of a shock as we was talking about the football at the time. God is dead? That's not true is it? If so, what's the point of it all?

If God does exist still, does he punish us for our past sins? I used to throw stones at the sally army as a boy.

please reply but dont send people round.

Harry Tartt.

CONTACT FOR **CHRIST**

Selsdon House, 212-220 Addington Road
South Croydon, Surrey CR2 8LD
Tel: 0181-651 6246   Fax: 0181-651 6429

Our ref: 2299-99/at

10 September, 1999

Mr Harry Tartt
26 Baildon Street
Deptford
LONDON
SE8 4BQ

Dear Mr Tartt

Thank you for writing to the *Public Transport Scripture Text Mission*, after seeing one of their adverts. PTSTM have passed your enquiry on to us, to deal with.

I am enclosing a free booklet entitled *Ten Myths About Christianity*, which, if you read it, will answer the questions in your letter.

If, after reading the booklet, you would like some further help, please fill in the enclosed reply-card and send it back to us. I hope that this is helpful to you.

Yours sincerely

Andrew Taylor

MICHAEL GREEN & GORDON CARKNER

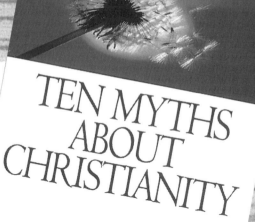

TEN MYTHS ABOUT CHRISTIANITY

LION

Furthe

If, after reading this bookl
through contact with a l
details below

✂ ------------------------------

22519-999

Mr/Mrs/Miss Harry Tartt   Age ~~9~~ 78

Address 26 Bailden street

Deptford

London   Post Code SE8 4BQ

Telephone

I would like (tick as appropriate)

☑ a Christian to write to me
☐ a Christian to telephone me

NO ✗ ~~a visit from a local Christian~~

Other details that you think might help us to help you
Will I go to hell for using bad language?
I have also in the past been known to have
looked at glamour magazines.
can I be forgiven? Or will I be smitten by god?

26 Baildon Street
Deptford
London SE8

Dear Christadelphian Information Service,

I was given your address by Andre, the painist at my local pub. Following a recent near-death experience involving a tram (the details are unimportant right now), I have been looking at the world in a new light. The other day as I was sat watching Kilroy I had a terrible sensation in my guts (at first I thought it was wind again), then I found myself shaking with fear and asking some very big questions like-

What happens when I die?

What's the point of it all?

Do I even exist?

Can you help me? I've never asked the meaningfull questions before.

Yours in hope,

Harry Tartt.

Roy Chessum
Advertising Secretary
Bexley [Dawn] Christadelphians

23rd August 1999

Mr H.Tartt
26 Baildon Street
Deptford
London
SE8

Dear Mr Tartt,

With reference to your message left on our Answer Phone herewith some booklets which I trust you will find of interest and will I am sure have the questions you are asking yourself..

Should you require any further booklets then please write to me at the above address.

Yours sincerely,

[signature: Roy Chessum]

Light ...

on t

Light on a New World

... a bi-monthly magazine which deals with the Bible's important message for today

Light

...ON A NEW WOR

Bible
Con
Co

What is
Death ?

ONE BIB
many chur
WHY?

'There is one body, and or
called in one ho
One Lord, on

LIGHT
ON YOU
FUTUR

AN INTRODUCT
OF THE MAGAZ
'LIGHT~ON A N

The truth about
HEAVEN
& HELL

The heaven, even the heavens, are the LORD'
but the earth hath he given to the childre
PSALM

26 Baildon Street
Deptford
London SE8 4BQ.

Butlins Holiday Camp,
Warren Road
Minehead
Somerset
TA24 5SH

Dear Head Of Butlins,

Although I had a rotten time at Butlins, this was no fault of yours. You see, my lady friend has been acting up of late and this reached a head when we had a weeks break at your camp. She ruined my big treat by barely speaking two words to me, and she never once laughed at any of my jokes. Indeed, the only time she would unpurse her lips was when the redcoat who looked like Kilroy joined us (she laughed at ALL his jokes, mind). That apart though, I have to say, on the whole the entertainment was wonderfull (even if she sat there with a face like thunder the whole time).

Now, I have a question for you. At 76 years, am I too old to become a redcoat? I come from a music-hall tradition you see. Perhaps youve heard of The Tumbling Tartts?

Please reply,

Harry Tartt. (Entertainments Manager, The Angry Toad Pubic House).

Butlins Family Entertainment Resort, Minehead, Somerset TA24 5SH
Tel: (01643) 703331 Fax: (01643) 705264

Mr Harry Tartt
26 Baildon Street
Deptford
London
SE8 4BQ

15 October 1999

Dear Mr Tartt

Thank you for your letter regarding your recent stay at Butlins Family
Entertainment Resort in Minehead.

I am afraid we are not recruiting for Redcoats at present but thank you for
the interest you have shown in our resort.

We wish you all the best for the future.

Yours sincerely

H. C. Crabb

Paul Beckett
Reds Academy Manager

BUTLINS LIMITED   A COMPANY WITHIN THE RANK GROUP PLC   REGISTERED IN ENGLAND NO. 323698   6 CONNAUGHT PLACE   LONDON W2

26 Baildon Street
Deptford
London Se8 4BQ

Dear Robert Kilroy Silk,

Although I must admit to having been a bit jealous of you in the past (my lady freind is obsessed with you), Ive decided to stop getting angry about it and treat it all as a joke. So I would greatly apreciate it if you would send a photo made out to "Mrs. Johnson", and signed by yourself. I think it might help our relationship. Could you put something about forgiving me on it?

Thanks now,

Harry Tartt.

26 Baildon Street

Deptford

London SE8 4Bq.

Dear Association Of Wrens,

I know this is a long shot but I wonder if you have a contact adress for a certain ex-wren who was close to my heart. Her name was Hilary Macivelry and she was the love of my life. If you cant give me her name, would you forward this letter and poem?

Hilary

Hilary Macivelry was an upright, handsome woman.
She made you proud to be around her heaving lips and pouting bosom.
She came from somewhere way up North, where apparently it always rained,
But she bought the sun to my young heart, then left it full of pain.

I danced with her at a services ball. I was drunk, yes, but not on vino
'Twas a keg of beer that made me leer, and destroy my chance with her, oh!
Yet still to this day I can see her face, and can feel her slender hips
But the one thing I shall always curse is I never kissed those lips.

I know Im a soppy old sod, but she has haunted my thoughts ever since. Get her adress or forward my poem please.

Yours in hope,

Harry Tartt.

THE ASSOCIATION OF WRENS

FOUNDED 1920

Patron:
H.R.H. THE PRINCESS ROYAL

Secretary:
Mrs E. J. Hardie

8 HATHERLEY STREET
LONDON SW1P 2YY
Telephone: 0171 932 0111

27th August 1999

Dear Mr Tartt,

Thank you for your letter with the poem for Hilary.

We regret we are unable to help in tracing your ex-Wren friend Hilary Macivelry as she is not a member of the Association. We have the facility on our computer to check under both single and married names but she doesn't appear on the record. We are therefore returning your letter along with information on other outlets for tracing old friends which you may not know about and may like to try.

We hope that you may have luck in finding Hilary.

Yours sincerely,

p.p. Secretary

Charity Registration No. 257040

SERVICE PALS

30 WORDS MAXIMUM ON POST CARD

INCLUDE YOUR OWN NAME AND ADDRESS

ONLY ONE SUBMISSION PER PERSON PER MONTH CONSIDERED

WRITE TO - SERVICE PALS, TELETEXT, PO BOX 297 LONDON SW6 1XT

FAX: 0171 381 8525

If you do find a long lost friend through SERVICE PALS, please let Channel 4 know

Write to Gail Gillogaley at the above address.

YOURS MAGAZINE — A MONTHLY MAGAZINE FOR THE OLDER PERSON RUN A FREE 'FIND A FRIEND' SERVICE. WE USED TO BE ABLE TO GIVE YOU THE ADDRESS TO WRITE TO BUT THEY HAVE CHANGED THEIR FORMAT AND NOW HAVE A COUPON WHICH HAS TO BE FILLED OUT WITH EACH APPEAL AND THEY WILL NOT ACCEPT PHOTOCOPIES OF THE COUPON. THE MAGAZINE COSTS 80p PER ISSUE AND DEVOTES THREE OR FOUR PAGES TO THIS SERVICE.

26 Baildon Street
Deptford
London SE8 4BQ.

dear Ann Widecombe MP.

Ann, I am a huge fan of yours, in fact I firmly beleive you could one day be the next
Prime Minister of this country. Now then, I know that you have some very firm views
on law and order and the young and what not - so let me tell you about the goings on
round our way. A young kid by the name of Kenny Pringle (barely out of short pants)
is running the roost. Its a joke. The worse part is, the police and teachers seem
powerless to do anything. I blame the liberal attitudes of Quentin Hogg and Ray
Jenkins in the 60's. Those chickens are now coming home to roost.

I have it on good authority (my companion is a dinner-lady at the local comprehensive)
that young Pringle was involved in a very serious incident at the school the other day.
Apparantley he locked the headmaster in the staff loos, then broke into his office,
barrackaded the doors and proceeded to make hay. Supposedley he broke into the
drinks cabinet, then broadcast rude words, reggay music and a whole episode of
supermarket sweep over the school tannoy system. This would have gone on a lot later
if two gym teachers hadn't broke down the barrickades and forcibly ejected him. The
worst thing is (and this makes me so mad) he is now attempting to sue the gym
teachers for manhandling him.

What can we do about this ridiculous situation? Who is in charge? What would you
do about it if you ever get back into power?

Id like a reply from you if thats alright.

Yours,

Harry Tartt.

HOUSE OF COMMONS
LONDON SW1A 0AA

Mr. Harry Tartt,
26 Basildon Street,
Deptford, London SE20 4BQ

7th September, 1999

Dear Mr. Tartt,

Ann Widdecombe is away from the office today and I am therefore writing in her absence to acknowledge receipt of your letter in which you express your serious concerns about the behaviour of Kenny Pringle. Miss Widdecombe will see all correspondence on her return and she may write to you herself at that time. She will be grateful to you for sharing this information with her.

It is appreciated that you have approached Miss Widdecombe about the general issue of lack of police power in circumstances such as those which you describe and she will note your comments with care and will bear them in mind in discussion with colleagues. However, it seems that help is needed locally to deal with the problem now and it would be appropriate for you to contact your own Member of Parliament, Ms Joan Ruddock, to ask for her help with this problem. You could write to her at the House of Commons or I am sure she has an office in the constituency where you could arrange to see her. I hope this is helpful.

Yours sincerely,

Charlotte Wallis

Mrs. C. Wallis,
Secretary/PA to Ann Widdecombe, MP

26 Baildon Street
deptford
London SE8 4BQ.

English Tourist board,
Thames Tower
Blacks Road
London W6 9EL

Dear Ros Carey,

Thank you for bothering to reply to my letter (which is more than the Welsh Tourist Board did). Whilst I understand what you said in your reply I think you are very wrong about encouraging the welsh to visit for free. However, before I continue Id like to make one point - I am not prejudiced, in fact some of my best freinds are Welsh! What I would say though is surely we already have enough tourists in London without adding to the problem. In fact no trip to the west End seems to be complete without me being sent sprawling by some tourist's day-glow napsack. It was only a few months back that I was insultingly mistaken for a Chelsea Pensioner by a hoard of Jap tourists (I think it was because I happened to be wearing the red over-coat that mrs. Johnson bought me). Surrounded by them, jabbering and taking photos of me, I panicked and swung my stick around to dispel the frenzied mob. Unfortunately it poked one of them in the eye and caused a bit of a diplomatic incident. Luckily the copper that removed me from the angry mob was quite understanding and gave me a cup of tea back at the station. A far cry from Z-Cars I thought.

Anyhow Ros, as far as London is concerned - would it be possible to reserve certain spaces for London residents and others for tourists? Id let them have Leicester Square and Picadilly Circus for instance, but would like back Westminster Abbey and Hyde park (where I always seem to get hit by American footballs!)

Thanks mate, look forward to your reply.

Harry Tartt.

ENGLISH
TOURISM
COUNCIL

Mr. Harry Tarrt
26 Baildon Street
Deptford
London SE8 4BQ

8 September 1999

Dear Mr. Tarrt

Direct Line: 0181 563 3394
Direct Fax: 0181 563 3350
rcarey@mail.bta.org.uk

Thank you for writing to me again.

I am sorry to learn that you were attacked by a frenzied mob of tourists but at least it proved that our policeman are wonderful. (We promote them as icons you know, along with red buses and red telephone boxes which we have to pretend still exist in profusion. People only find out when they get here that they don't and then it's too late!)

Anyway – do you think you may have dreamt this incident? It does have an odd ring to it. You do not sound old enough to be mistaken for a Chelsea Pensioner. On the other hand, a reference to Z Cars rather than The Bill does date you a bit!

Turning to your suggestion that certain parts of London be reserved for residents: I think many Londoners would agree with you. We do not of course! Also, there is a little piece of legislation called the Race Relations Act standing in the way!

Yours sincerely,

Ros Carey
Head of Policy

PS: Who is Mrs. Johnson? Surely not Dr. Johnson's wife if she recently gave you a coat. Is this the name that Mrs. Tarrt goes by?

PPS: I hope you are not writing a book in the manner of Henry Root.

English Tourism Council, Thames Tower, Black's Road, London W6 9EL
Telephone (020) 8563 3000 Facsimile (020) 8563 0302 www.englishtourism.org.uk
English Tourism Council – Incorporated under the Development of Tourism Act 1969 as English Tourist Board

26 Baildon Street

Deptford

London SE8 4BQ.

Dear Graham Mackrell (West Ham United Club Secretary),

Although I dont like football myself (I live close to Millwall), my old dad was a big footie fan. He used to support the hammers with a passion bordering on madness. He actualy attended the famous Wembley final of 1923 when the copper had to clear the pitch of fans. In fact his claim to fame was that the famous White Horse peed on his shoe . Recentley I found the shoe in an old box labelled "The White Horse Final". So what I want to know is - would you like it for the West Ham Museum? I dont want the bloody thing, you'd be more than welcome to it. Please let me know and enclose postage if you do want it (or pay for my transport down to you).

Could you also send me a picture of the historic final? Maybe of the white horse itself?

Cheers now,

Harry Tartt. Pensioner.

Our Ref: GHM/HT/CAH

3rd September 1999

Mr H Tartt
26 Baildon Street
Deptford
London
SE8 4BQ

Dear Mr Tartt,

Thank you for your recent letter regarding your treasured possession of your father's shoe from the White Horse Cup Final.

We would love to have this amongst our possessions and should be most grateful if you could arrange for it to be forwarded to us.

We will of course settle by return any costs involved.

Kind regards.

Yours sincerely,

Graham Mackrell
Company Secretary

WEST HAM UNITED FOOTBALL CLUB PLC

REGISTERED OFFICE: BOLEYN GROUND, GREEN STREET, UPTON PARK, LONDON E13 9AZ
Telephone: 020 8548 2748 Facsimile: 020 8548 2758 www.westhamunited.co.uk Registration No.66516

26 Baildon Street
Deptford
London SE8 4BQ.

Dear Graham Mackrell (West Ham United Club Secretary),

Thanks for your speedy reply Graham, must be pretty keen to get your hands on that shoe, eh? I dont blame you mate, dont blame you at all - it's historic is that shoe. But lets cut the sweet talk and get down to brass tacks (as my Uncle Joan used to say). I know as well as you do that neither of us are business men, but what we are is men of the world Graham. We know how it works - you scratch my back and all that. Now what I'm suggesting is maybe a little "thank you" (to cover the emotional wrench of parting with said shoe). I was thinking a small sum of money - say £150 ? Doesnt sound too much to me - you can even have the original shoe box. I dont want you to think I'm a wide boy Graham, I'm more like what The English Tourist Board described me as - "an entrepeneur".

Get in touch, we'll talk,

Harry Tartt. Pensioner.

Our Ref: GHM/HT/CAH

8th September 1999

Mr H Tartt
26 Baildon Street
Deptford
London
SE8 4BQ

Dear Mr Tartt,

Thank you for your latest letter regarding the famous shoe.

It has been suggested that we subject the shoe to a DNA test to make sure it is an original.

I wonder how we can now progress this situation?

Yours sincerely,

Graham Mackrell
Company Secretary

WEST HAM UNITED FOOTBALL CLUB PLC

REGISTERED OFFICE: BOLEYN GROUND, GREEN STREET, UPTON PARK, LONDON E13 9AZ
Telephone: 020 8548 2748 Facsimile: 020 8548 2758 www.westhamunited.co.uk Registration No.66516

26 baildon street
Deptford
London SE8 4BQ.

Graham Mackrell (West Ham United Club Secretary),

Regarding the shoe.

Dear Graham,

Im a little bit upset that you think I need a DNA test. I fought in the war and was injured in Palermo you know. Im not about to go and pee on an old loafer and try and fob it off as The White Horse Shoe, its just not in my nature. Still, I appreciate that these days you can never be too carefull. I should know, I was sold a watch on Deptford High Street which actually exploded on the stroke of 12, it frightened the bloody life out of me (I missed out on a Full House as well). Still, I digress - what I want to tell you Graham is, I am still open to offers but Billy Baxter (who is acting on my behalf) has advised me to aproach Wembley Stadium with the historic artifact, and I am sure that once they get a sniff of the shoe theyll be very eager to rid me of it! He also advised aproaching Preston North End but I dont have their adress. Do you? Perhaps you could give it me, because Ive only got a <u>London</u> Directory.

Thanks Graham, and Id hurry if I was you, Baxter reckons there could well be a bidding war for the shoe.

Get in touch,

Harry tartt.

P.S. Good luck to your team, I hope they fare better in Europe than I did.

NO REPLY.

26 Baildon Street
deptford
London
SE8 4Bq.

Dear Sophie and Prince Edward of Wessex,

Congratulations, sincere congratulations on what was in my book the marriage of the decade (bigger than beckham and Spice). Congrats and best of luck to you both, you'll need it - what with press intrusions and what not. Anyway for now, rejoice, rejoice!

Unfortunately, and here's the rub - I missed the whole blooming thing, as the day before I'd accidentaly knocked over my telly during a particularly smarmy edition of The Kilroy Show. So, in all deference, I ask you for a photo of you the happy couple. Is it possible to sign it?

Thanks very much,

Harry Tartt (war veteran).

P.S. is it true that the queen (your mother-in-law Sophie) had to queue for beef Stew at the reception? Times have certaiNly changed. Thanks in advance for the photo

From: Lieutenant Colonel Sean O'Dwyer, LVO

BUCKINGHAM PALACE

24th September, 1999.

Dear Mr Tartt,

The Earl and Countess of Wessex have asked me to thank you very much indeed for your kind letter.

In response to your request for a photograph, I am afraid that we have no official pictures of Their Royal Highnesses since their wedding for distribution.

I am sorry to have to send you this disappointing reply.

Yours sincerely

Sean O'Dwyer

Private Secretary to TRH The Earl and Countess of Wessex

Harry Tartt, Esq.

26 Baildon Street
Deptford
London SE8 4BQ.

Dear Colonel Sean O'Dwyer c/o Buckingham Palace,

Having recentley recieved a letter from the Palace, your name jumped right out and slapped me square in the face. Are you by any chance related to Colonel O'Dwyer who was posted in Palermo during the war? His first name was Sandie, I recall. He was my Colonel you see, and I looked up to him a lot, regardless of his drinking.

Many years after his unfortunate dicharge, we took to playing tennis together on a regular basis in Greenwich. Sadly, after securing a rare victory against the Colonel, I attempted to jump the net to shake hands. Unfortunately I became entangled in the net, and received whiplash to the groin. I was unable to continue with the tennis, and we unfortunatly lost contact. That was back in 1967 I think. Could you let me know if hes a relative of yours? Also could you let me know if he's still alive? I'd love to hear from you as I'M planning a re-union party for some of my old pals. Youd be welcome to come, weather or not you are related. It'll be in my local pub in Deptford.

I look forward to your letter Colonel,

Your humble servant,

Harry Tartt.

From: Lieutenant Colonel Sean O'Dwyer LVO

BUCKINGHAM PALACE

27th October 1999

Dear Mr Tarld,

No I'm sorry to tell you that I am no relation to Colonel Sandie O'Dwyer and to be honest I have not heard of him — pity as he sounds a colourful character.

Sorry to disappoint you.

Yours sincerely,

Sean O'Dwyer.

London SW1A 1AA Tel: 0171 930 4832 Fax: 0171 930 8462

26 Baildon Street
Deptford
LONDON Se8 4BQ

Dear Princes Trust,

I have always very admired the work what the Prince Of wales has done with the less priviliged kids with the problems they have with litracy and such like.
So what Id like to do is nominate someone for a spell in The Princes Trust to learn the value and importance of not being a right little git and hooligan. The person to who I refer is Kenny Pringle - and he is getting right on my wick . For a couple of years now our estate has been under seige from the likes of him.
Kenny Pringle is barely into his teens, yet he recentley drove to the Deptford Job Center aboard a motorised lawn mower (which looked suspiciously like one nicked from a local park). As he drove down the road he proudly waved to all the shoppers on the high street (some of whom waved back). Pleased as punch he was. He didnt care a hoot about the traffic jam he caused. Or the grass flying out the back of the mower (which covered the likes of me and other pensioners).

Can you enlist him soon? You had better write to me as his mother's a lush, and his dad done a moonlit flit.

Hes off the rails but I dont think he's rotten through and through.

Yours sincereley

Harry Tartt.

NO REPLY

26 Baildon Street
Deptford
London Se8 4BQ.

Dear Nick Raynsford MP,

Having just been told that Greenwich is to be an exclusion zone on Old Years Night, I have just hot-footed it back from the pub to lodge my protest. As a resident of Deptford I am just spitting distance from Greenwich, yet although a South Londoner for all my seventy odd years, I am to be barred from the big milenium party. A very socialist attitude I must say! I suppose us infriors in deptford will have to make do with a couple of soggy bangers and a mini-riot. Thanks a lot. Shame on you Mr. Raynsford. And to think you want us to vote for you as Mayor of London!

I wont expect a reply as your probably too busy ringing your important friends, and organising the catering for your big party.

Yours,

Harry Tartt.

NICK RAYNSFORD MP

HOUSE OF COMMONS
LONDON SW1A 0AA
Office 020 7219 5895
020 7219 2773
Fax 020 7219 2619

5 October 99

Dear Mr Tartt,

I am afraid that you are not accurate in your assumptions about access to Greenwich Town Centre. The over-riding issue is one of safety and and ensuring a safe environment for people living in Greenwich and wishing to come to the Town Centre to celebrate the millennium.

There have been serious discussions involving the Police and Emergency Services, local authority and local people on how to ensure good organisation of the various events being held in the town on 31 December. We have seen in the past the dangerous crushes which have occurred in Trafalgar Square and have learned from events like the Notting Hill Carnival and Edinburgh's Hogmany Celebrations on how best to manage these events. Advice will be given on the basis of experience gleaned from these events to local residents in due course.

Yours sincerely,

Nick Raynsford MP

Mr H Tartt
26 Baildon Street
Deptford
London SE8 4BQ

26 Baildon street
Deptford
London SE8 4BQ.

House Of Commons
Westminster
London SW1.

Dear Teresa Gorman,

I am writing to you because you are one of the few M.P's who make sense to me. I want to tell you that I have been greatly inflamed by events surrounding British Beef. I beleive the French are firing warning shots across our bows and we need to answer back with our big guns. Once again The Angry Toad Public House has decided to fight back. We are organising a charabanc to France, which will be decked out in Union Jacks. Whilst in Calais we will be dressed as famous British historical figures, and eating beef-steaks in front of the French people (weather they like it or not).

I'm proud to be British and will be dressed as Henry The Eighth. Its all good fun, but theres a serious point behind it all - WE SIMPLY CANT AFFORD TO BE DRAGGED AROUND BY THE BRUSSELS

BUREAUCRATS.

We would appreciate a message of support.

Yours as always,

H. Tartt.

Harry Tartt.

Dear Harry,
How I wish I could come too! You have my full support & my best wishes

Teresa

26 Baildon Street

Deptford

London SE8 4BQ.

Dear Tramtrack Croydon Ltd,

I am writing to you for reassurance about the safety of your trams. A frightning thing happened to me recentley,when I took my lady friend to Blackpool to try and cheer her up. We was dis-embarking from a tram when one of my braces got hooked inside the door. I banged on the side of the tram in terror as the doors closed shut, but was drowned out by a nearby brass band. The tram then took off, with me attatched to it by my braces. I found myself running alongside the tram using all my effort to keep up (I'm in My Seventies). I kept expecting the driver to stop but he just kept hurtling along. In fact I had to run half the length of the golden Mile before he stopped and I could quickly unhook and release myself.

Now although this seems to have caused great amusement to every body (not least my lady-friend), I keep having panic attacks and flash-backs.

I will soon be visiting Croydon and might need to use the tram, can you assure me of its safety?

Yours,

Harry Tartt.

Tramtrack Croydon Ltd

92 Addiscombe Road **Tel: 0181-662 9800**
Croydon   Fax: 0181-662 9810
Surrey
CR0 5PP

TCL

27 October 1999

Our Ref : 1131/271099c.ct/kp

Mr H Tartt
26 Basildon Street
Deptford
London
SE8 4BQ

Dear Mr Tartt

Many thanks for your recent letter concerning your 'near accident' on the Blackpool system.

Firstly let me say how sorry I was to hear of your misfortune and reassure you that this type of incident would be most unlikely to be replicated on our system.

The safety of the public including our own passengers is of the utmost priory for Tramtrack Croydon Limited.

Indeed our whole system including vehicle design and safety is subject to the most rigorous safety approvals regime by the Health and Safety Executive.

Even so, such 'high level' risks are subject to regular internal review to ensure that the control measures produce a residual risk that is as low as reasonably practicable.

I trust this fully answers any concerns you had.

Yours sincerely
for and on behalf of
Tramtrack Croydon Limited

Brian Johns
Project Director

Registered Office: 92 Addiscombe Road, Croydon, Surrey CR0 5PP
Registered in England and Wales No. 3092613   VAT No. 672 7555 05

26 Baildon Street
Deptford
London SE8 4BQ

Matthew Gerard Travel Insurance Ltd,
7 Westminster Court
Hipley Street
Old Woking.
GU22 9LQ

Dear Matthew,

I know you normally deal with insurance for abroad, but can you tell me, is it possible to take out insurance for traveling in Britain, on Railtrack?

Yours sincerely,

Harry Tartt.

NO REPLY.

26 Baildon Street
Deptford
London Se8 4BQ.

Dear Mike Read,

'Ave a word my son! Seriously though, I am a huge fan of yours - huge. I saw you once at Lewisham Theater and wet myself laughing (literaly). Personally I put you up there with Max Miller and dear old Ken Calhoun - very funny indeed, very funny. I am greatly looking forward to my library getting a big print copy of your autobiography "T'rific" (I spend a lot of time in the library now I dont have a lady-friend). Meantime could you send us a photo inscribed to me with a catch-phrase of yours such as "Ricky!".

Keep doing what you do best my son,

Harry tartt. Pensioner.

Good Luck Harry
.. "Ricky.." !
all the best -
Mike Read.

26 Baildon Street
Deptford
London SE8 4BQ.

Dear Jeffrey Archer,

I was very pleased to receive your package, it bought a real smile to my face, and before I forget, well done on getting nominated for Mayor - now it really begins. Beleive me, its only a matter of time before Norris bites the dust, then (God-willing) you'll be in the ring going toe-to-toe with Glenda Jackson, I for one would like to be ring-side for THAT. To be honest I thought that your biggest threat was Red Ken, but I reckon his own party will do for him. So, the way I see it is, Jeffrey Archer Versus Glenda Jackson for the crown of London. My advice Jeffrey is take the gloves off, get your hands dirty - throw some dirt. Beleive me, theres plenty of stuff that shes done that she wont like being reminded of. Christ, Im suprised she didnt take her clothes off to do Morcambe and Wise! (It was about the only time she didn't).

Do you think I could I be employed in some capacity (perhaps in publicity, or as press spokesman?) Im a real Londoner, born and bread. Please let me know, I need to be doing something, other than going to the local library or sitting on a bench. I want to help.

Yours in hope,

Harry Tartt.

JEFFREY ARCHER

Harry Tartt Esq.
26 Basildon Street
Deptford
London
SE8 4BQ

REF: CK/CO

1st November 1999

Dear Harry

Thank you for your letter to Jeffrey which has been passed onto me as Chief of Staff. I must apologise for the delay in getting back to you but I have been away on business.

We would of course greatly value your advice but we are not in a position to offer any employment as our key positions have already been filled.

If you have any further queries please do not hesitate to contact me or my secretary Camilla Kleeman.

Kind regards

Stephan Shakespeare
<u>Chief of Staff</u>

26 Baildon Street
Deptford
London S.E.8 4BQ.

BBC Telivision,
Television Center
Wood Lane
London W12 7RJ.

Dear Customer Enquiries,

If I was to de-tune BBC1 and BBC2 on my telly, would that mean I wouldnt have to pay the license fee anymore?

I look forward to your reply,

Mr. H. Tartt.

BBC Information

Mr H Tartt
26 Baildon Street
Deptford
London
SE8 4BQ

Our Ref 1981936

4 November 1999

Dear Mr Tartt

Thank you for your recent letter with your enquiry on television licensing. Please accept my apologies for the delay in replying.

The licence represents permission under the law to use television-receiving equipment. If the equipment is used solely for replaying pre-recorded video tapes, and a written assurance to this effect is provided to TV Licensing by the householder, a licence is not required. We would probably insist that equipment is modified so that it is no longer capable of receiving conventional broadcast signals. Householders would have to demonstrate to enquiry officers that their television is not being used to view broadcast programmes. If you wish to do so, you should write to the following address, remembering to give the assurances as set out above.

TV Licensing
Bristol
BS98 1TL

Thank you again for taking the time to write to us with your enquiry.

Yours sincerely

Jacqui MacDonald
BBC Information

26 Baildon STREET
Deptford
LoNdon SE8 4BQ.

Dear head Of Channel 5,

Can you please explain to me Chanel 5's obsession with Abba? Every time I turn on your channel its either someone doing an impression of them, or the godawful Abba themselfs. Whats it all about? An __ABBA DAY__???? Im sure Im not alone in thinking Abba were bloody awful the first time round. My advice to you is, if youre going to wallow in nostalgia at least pick something worthwhile, like Matt Monro, the late Frankie Vaughan, or even Old One Eye himself - Kenny Calhoun. Could that be arranged?

How about repeating The Good Old Days? or The Black and White Minstrels? Why not repeat The Dick Emery Show? The Army Game? Or More Tea Vicar? Anything but bloody Abba.

Come on Chanel 5, try harder.

Yours,

Mr. H. Tartt.

P.s. Could you repeat Confessions Of A Driving Instructor? Thanks.

Your Reference: DO/12652/PP/C12E

Date: 5th November 1999

Mr H Tarff
26 Basildon Street
Depford
London
SE8 4BQ

Dear Mr Tarff

Thank you for your recent letter.

We are not quite sure what you mean by 'Channel 5's obsession with ABBA?". **ABBA DAY** on the 10th October was the first time we have transmitted any programmes about ABBA since our launch.

We do appreciate that you are not a fan of ABBA, but the millions who tuned in to the day more than likely were.

We have made a note of the programmes you suggest we purchase. However, although these may have been successful for other channels, this doesn't automatically make them viable for Channel 5. We have a much smaller budget than the other terrestrial broadcasters and have overcome this disadvantage by offering programmes and schedules that are desirably different to those of our competitors.

Channel 5's identity has developed since launch and we now offer a genuine alternative to the other channels. We've got so much good programming of our own coming up, it is very unlikely that we'd be interested in old shows from the other channels.

Unfortunately, we do not have the rights to repeat **CONFESSIONS OF A DRIVING INSTRUCTOR** as we have already transmitted this film three times within our current contract.

Please note that the contact details for the Channel 5 Duty Office are as follows:

Telephone:	0845 7 05 05 05
Textphone:	0845 7 41 37 87
E mail:	dutyoffice@channel5.co.uk
Fax:	0171 550 5678

And the Channel 5 website can be found at www.channel5.co.uk

Thank you for your interest in Channel 5.

Yours sincerely

DUTY OFFICER

Channel 5 Broadcasting Limited 22 Long Acre London WC2E 9LY

Telephone: 0171 550 5555 Facsimile: 0171 550 5554

Registered in England no. 3147640

26 Baildon Street
Deptford
London SE8 4BQ.

Channel 5 Broadcasting Limited,
22 Long Acre
LONDON
WC2E 9LY.

Dear Frank Bruno,

I am so pleased to see you back on T.V. Frank, I was especially pleased as you said you was going to leave Britain if Labour got in at the last election (I was under the impression you had!) The other week I thanked my lucky stars as I watched Jim Davidson on The Generation Game, Phil Collins in a documentry about himself, and you in It's A Knockout - I thought "Thank God they all went back on their word!" There is a big enough drain of talent from this country as it is.

So please write to assure me that you'll stay put if the labour get a second term, and please send a photo of yourself with a funny quip. (My first name's 'Arry!).

Nice one Frank,

'Arry Tartt.

Best Wishes
from...
Shuri "

Mr Arry Tartt
26 Bazildon Street
Deptford
London SE8 4BQ

26 Baildon Street
Deptford
London SE8 4BQ.

Dear BBC,

Id just like to have confirmation of something if thats alright with you - the majority of my license fee _IS_ being spent on sending celebrity chef's around the world isn't it? Im pretty sure on this point but would just like confirmation. I'm all for sending Ainsley Harriot to the far flung corners of the globe, I just dont want to watch him cooking when he gets there. I also resent paying for his accomodation and return flight.

If we do have to pay for him to go abroad, I wish hed have the good manners to stay there.

Yours,

Harry Tartt. (Pensioner)

British Broadcasting Corporation PO Box 1116 Belfast BT2 7AJ Telephone 08700 100 222 Fax 01232 326453 E-Mail info@bbc.co.uk

BBC Information

Mr Harry Tartt
26 Baildon Street
Deptford
London
SE8 4BQ

Our Ref 2044309

17 November 1999

Dear Mr Tartt

Thank you for your recent letter concerning cookery programmes on BBC Television. Please accept my apologies for the delay in replying.

I regret to read that you are unhappy with such programmes, in particular the use of licence fee money to send chefs abroad. Working abroad on location is often more difficult than working on location in the UK and it is not a holiday for any of those involved. If the presenters have given an impression of 'holiday-making' in the process, it is actually a compliment to the professionalism of the reporters and film crew.

I am sorry that such programmes are not to your taste. Such programmes are, however, popular with a large number of our viewers and while we understand and are more than aware of your concerns, we must make it clear that we show the range of programmes which is expected of us from the wide and diverse audience we serve.

Thank you for taking the trouble to contact us.

Yours sincerely

Aileen Gallagher
BBC Information

26 Baildon Street
Deptford
London SE8 4BQ.

Dear Jimmy Young,

sorry to bother you but Id appreciate an answer on something if thats alright with you.
My old dad always maintained that my Uncles, who was in a performing troupe known
as The Tumblin' Tartts appeared on the same edition of Jukebox Jury as you.
Apparently they sung "Keep on Tumblin'" (it was voted a "miss" unfortunately).
However, behind the scenes there was supposedley an incident involving them and The
Beverley Sisters. Do you have any recolection of this?
I know that David Jacobs has refused to talk about it ever sinse.

Could you also tell me why you never released any other songs after "Unchained
Melody".

I look forward to hearing from you. (My radio's on the blink after it fell out my
window.)

Yours faithfully,

Harry Tartt.

NO REPLY

26 Baildon street
Deptford
London Se8 4BQ.

Dear Ned Sherrin,

Before I start I'd just like to say that I don't listen to Radio 4. I'm more a Radio 2 man myself, but the other day my wireless went up the spout and I was forced to listen to your programm. Within minutes I was howling with mirth, God what laughs! Although the programme occasionaly slipped into smugness, generaly it was good, clean, wholesome fun. In fact, it reminded me of an old 40's programme, "Pardon Me, Aunty" which featured Kenny Calhoun And The Catford Crooners. It was by far the best turn on the old Services Radio - maybe you recall it. Any road up, please pass my regards on to Arthur Smith, he's one for the future isn't he?

However Ned, what I wanted to ask you was - did I see you on Peckham High street the other day with whom I presume to have been your wife? You was wearing a sort of orange jogging suit and white plimsoles. Was it you? if so, I was the fellow who pulled the drunk off your wife. If it was you, could you send me a photo of yourself with a witty inscription? if it wasn't you, could you still send me a photo with a witty inscription?

Cheers Ned,

Harry Tartt.

Dear Mr Tartt,
Thankyou for your
unsigned letter (typed)
No - No wife
- 40 odd years since I was in
Peckham High Street.
- No jogging suit
- No plimsoles.
It sounds like Arthur

26 Baildon STREET

Deptford

London SE8 4BQ.

Dear Theatre Royal Haymarket,

On Wednesday night I was fortunate to attend your theatre for the opening night of "The Importance Of being earnest" with patricia Routlidge from Keeping Up Appearances. Unbeknownst to me the wonderful Queen Mother was in attendance on what was the 99th anniversary of her birth. Her radiant dis-position, and lusty laugh positively enlightened the whole night. the audience cheered and clapped like nobody's business upon her entrance and it was grand. I myself shouted "Hurrah!" and threw my cap in the air, but in the hullabaloo it never came down. I think it might have got caught in the lighting rig.

Was it handed in? It's a grey cloth cap with my name stitched in the inside.

Please reply as I am an old age pensioner and can ill afford the postage, let alone the loss of a good cap.

yours faithfully,

THEATRE ROYAL
HAYMARKET

Mr. Tartt,

Regretably your cap has not been found.

WITH COMPLIMENTS
THEATRE ROYAL HAYMARKET LIMITED, LONDON SW1Y 4HT
TELEPHONE (Management) 0171 930 8890 (Box Office) 0171 930 8800 Fax 0171 321 0139
A MEMBER OF THE LOUIS I. MICHAELS THEATRE GROUP OF COMPANIES

26 Baildon Street
Deptford
London SE8 4BQ.

Dear Pat Coombs,

Ive been trying to track you down for weeks. I wonder if you would do me a favour?
Could you send me a picture of yourself with an inscription which sounds like you
know me? You see, to get out of a tricky situation with my pals, I told them that I
was aquanted with you. Im sorry that I lied, but I had to think sharpish as they wanted
to remove my strides for charity!!!!

Id really appreciate it Pat. Thanks in advance,

Harry Tartt. Pensioner.

Dear Harry—

IT was nice to hear from you again... it's been a long time since our paths crossed!— P'raps you could get to see our radio series if we do another lot next year--? "Like They've Never Been Gone" has been great fun—& The 2nd series has recently gone out on R:4.— lovely to work with ——→

HARRODS!

With Compliments

Pat Coombs

HAPPY XMAS! to Harry~ Love & wishes
Patty C.

June W: & Roy Hudd again! so—cross your fingers for 2000 & hope we can enjoy a natter—!

HAVE A LOVELY XMAS! & a happy, healthy Millennium!

Pat!

26 BaiLdon Street
Deptford
LONDON SE8 4BQ.

BBC Telivision
Television Center
Wood Lane
London W12 7RJ

Dear BBC,

With regards the big millenium New Years Eve party - I have to tell you that I for one will be staying in. After being informed that my lady friend will be spending the night else where, my plans extend to sitting in my chair, drinking some light ale, and eating some cold cuts. There fore, on Old Years Night, I would like to see on television some good old traditional fare, like in the old days. Is it possible, I wonder, to bring back Andy Stewart, as I like to watch a good old highland Fling, or a jig and reeel. Although Im English, I do like to watch the Scots and Irish getting tanked up and celebrating as only they can. Hogmany should be left to the likes of Andy Stewart, Stanley Baxter, and Val Doonican - now <u>that</u> sounds like a party worth televising! Or dont you care about the older folk?

Let me know if this can be arranged.

Look forward to your reply,

Mr. H. Tartt.

P.S. I once saw Gordon Jackson attempt a sword dance when he was a bit "worse for wear". He was doing fine till he lost his balance and pulled a table full of sandwiches on top of himself. The bride-groom was livid. It was funny!

BBC Information

Mr H Tartt
26 Baildon Street
Deptford
London
SE8 4BQ

Our Ref 2044301

17 November 1999

Dear Mr Tartt

Thank you for your recent letter regarding programmes to be shown on BBC Television for the Millenium. Please accept my apologies for the delay in replying.

Please be assured that your comments have been carefully registered and forwarded on to the relevant departments for consideration, although I cannot guarantee that your request will be met.

Thank you again for taking the time and trouble to write to the BBC with your comments.

Yours sincerely

Clare Kenna

Jacqui MacDonald
BBC Information

26 Baildon Street
Deptford
London Se8 4BQ.

Dear Scottish Tourist Board,

What I wanT to talk about is the behavior of your <u>fans</u> during the England Scotland match. Just as the game began, our pub was invaded by Scottish football supporters (all of whom was tanked up). I have to say I found their behaviour less than acceptable. Until their arrival I had been quite happy, if a little quiete - but that was soon to change. One of the tartan yobbos spent the whole of the match playing his bagpipes right in my ear (and Ive got terrible tinitus after an accident in Morocco!). Another of the yobbos pinched my cap and replaced it with a ginger wig - which everyone found hilarious. Finally, when I went to the loo at the end of the match one of the Scots remarked (for the benifit of the whole pub) that mine was the best English tackle hed seen all night. The fact that my ex-lady friend was in the pub sitting with my ex-best freind, Billy Baxter, made me very embarassed.

This night saddened me as I previously had nothing against the Scots.

Yours,

Harry Tartt.

NO REPLY

26 Baildon Street
Deptford
London SE8 4BQ.

BBC Television.

Dear BBC,

In light of us pensioners now getting our license fees paid, I would like to congratulate the BBC on doing a fine job.

I beleive the BbC is a fine institution with ground-breaking programming such as Airport and all the decorating shows. Well done and can I have a picture of Gregg Dyke?

Yours Sinserely,

Mr. Harold Tartt.

tish Broadcasting Corporation PO Box 1116 Belfast BT2 7AJ Telephone 08700 100 222 Fax

BBC Information

Mr Harold Tartt
26 Baildon Street
Deptford
London
SE8 4BQ

Our Ref 2118122

3 December 1999

Dear Mr Tartt

Thank you for your recent letter regarding BBC Television. Please accept my apologies for the delay in replying.

It was kind of you to write to us with your appreciation of the BBC and I will forward your compliments to all concerned. I have also enclosed some information from BBC Online about Greg Dyke.

Thank you once again for taking the trouble to contact us in this way.

Yours sincerely

Joanne Gurney
BBC Information

BBC: Executive Committee

Greg Dyke was appointed **BBC Director-General Designate** in June 1999. He joins the Corporation on 1st November, 1999 and becomes Director-General on 1st April 2000.

Greg Dyke was born on 20 May 1947 in West London. Initially a newspaper journalist, he went on to study politics at York University from 1971. In 1977 he joined London Weekend Television as a reporter on The London Programme, became a producer on Weekend World in 1978 and then Deputy Editor of The London Programme in 1979. In 1981 he created and then became editor of The Six O'Clock Show.

Greg Dyke was appointed Editor-in Chief at breakfast television station TV-am in 1983 and in 1984 joined TVS (Television South) as Director of Programmes. He rejoined LWT in 1987 (Television South) as Director of was a Director of Channel Four Television from 1988 as Director of March 1990 he became LWT's Managing the ITN (Indepe...

26 Baildon Street
Deptford
London SE8 4BQ.

Dear Lewisham Council,

First off, thankyou for not replying to my letter about the litter.

Secondly, I want to say that we, the people of Deptford, are under attack. Under attack from grafiti artists (and I use the word "artists" wrongly). Anthing that stays still for over two minutes now is being "tagged" (as they call it) - buildings, parked cars, on one occasion they even tagged a milk-float! A lovely old fellow I know, named Alfie Crum, recentley had his motorized cart scribbled on after hed mistakenly fallen asleep in Brockwell Park.

If it was up to me Id issue them with a wire brush and spirits and get them to clean up the whole area, but I suppose you lot would probably offer them a chocolate biscuit and counselling!! Then again, as I watched a swan struggling with a McDonalds box the other day, I thought how unlike the council it would be to have a clean-up campaign. After all, why should the council care about how the place looks? I'm being sarcastic.

Yours not expecting a reply,

Mr. Harry Tartt. Pensioner.

Bizarre Court Scuffle

Court proceedings were interrupted yesterday when an elderly man burst into Greenwich Magistrates Court, and attempted to assault the defendant with a coal shovel. Amid gasps of surprise, the senior citizen was roughly bundled to the floor and forcibly ejected from the courtroom. The defendant tried to have the trial annulled, but to no avail.

Kenny Pringle, 17, of 51b McCaulliffe Street, Deptford, was found guilty of master-minding a campaign of graffiti in and around the Deptford area. Slogans daubed on walls and shop-fronts ranged from the bizarre 'Legalise Beef Cobbler' to the mysterious 'Harry Tartt is Innocent.' Sentencing was postponed for social reports.

Lewisham

Executive Director for Regeneration: Joseph Montgomery

Cleansing Services
Wearside Service Centre
Wearside Road
Lewisham
London SE13 7EZ

Telephone (020) 8690 4366
Fax (020) 8314 2043

Our Ref: ST/109/99

Mr Harry Tartt
26 Baildon Road
Deptford
London
SE8 4BQ

13 December 1999

Dear Mr Tartt

Thank you for your recent letter.

Firstly, I would like to advise you that I never received your initial letter regarding litter and therefore, I was unable to reply to you. I can only apologise for the disappointment you experienced in relation to this matter.

Secondly, I can fully appreciate your concerns with the graffiti in the Borough and in particular, Deptford. The council agree that it is not acceptable and we are in the process of actioning 'clean-up campaigns'. Town centres are the first port of call and the teams have already visited Blackheath, Catford and Forest Hill. Lewisham town centre is planned for next week, with Deptford and New Cross taking place in the New Year. The clean-up sessions include graffiti removal, mechanical sweeping for the road and pavements, collection of large items, weeding and assessing paving problems.

Furthermore, Lewisham Council is taking part in the 'National Spring Clean Campaign' run by the Tidy Britian Group. This is planned to take place in April 2000.

I am pleased to advise you that we have recently recruited an Enforcement Team who are prosecuting offenders of environmental crime. It is their intention to prosecute fly-tippers, dog owners who allow their dogs to foul on public areas and at least 5 graffiti vandals, before March 2000.

Lastly, we are encouraging our 'Street Leaders' (team of people who voluntary assist the Council) to clean graffiti from their own private property. The Council provides the equipment and training necessary for the Street Leaders to remove the graffiti themselves. If you would like further information with regards to this scheme, please do not hesitate to call me on 018 314 2109.

Contd/....

Mayor for Lewisham: Councillor Dave Sullivan   VAT Registration No. 205 5960 69

Thank you for taking the time to write to us with your comments and I hope you feel reassured that we are making every effort to improve our environment.

Yours sincerely

26 Baildon Street
Deptford
London Se8 4BQ.

Radio 2
Broadcasting House
London W1A 1AA

Dear Steve Wright,

I am just writing to say what a breath of fresh air you are on Radio 2 and I am full of admiration for what you do (your "craft" if you like). The skill to carry on talking regardless is a hard one to learn, as I can testify. I had a disastrous stint as a D.J. while in the army (I was sacked for only playing The Inkspots).

The reason I am writing is to ask if you are related to bob "Chalky" White who was a jockey on the old forces networK. He was later sacked for adding swear words to Anthony Eden's speeches (like you, he was a real loose cannon!) Apparentley he was the inspiration behind "Good Morning Vietnam" - though they changed it quite a lot ("Good Afternoon Cairo" doesnt sound quite the same does it?)

Please write and let me know.

Cheers now,

Harry Tartt (signing off)

NO REPLY

Fortune theater,
Russel Street
London WC2.

26 Baildon Street
Deptford
London Se8 4BQ.

Dear Theater Manger,

I recentley won two tickets in a raffle to see "The Woman In Black", and jumped at the chance to attend a big West end Show. Now, unfortunatly I wasnt aware it was a ghost story, and was not prepared for the horror that un-folded before my eyes. I have to tell you that I was made to jump on several occasions and unfortunately had a bit of an accident where I sat. Luckily I had a bag containing a spare pair of trousers and managed a quick change in the lavs during the interval. The thing being, I think I left my cap behind in the W.C. - was it handed in? Its a cloth cap with my name stitched on the inside (H. Tartt.) . Id appreciate it if youd let me know, so I can come up and collect it. Also I wonder if you should warn old folk about coming to see your show, as many of us suffer from delicate afflictions. I know that Alfie Crum had a similar experience when he went to see Cliff Richards as Heathcliff.

I look forward to your reply.

Yours sincerly,

Harry Tartt.

M.A.P. International Ltd.
Fortune Theatre, Russell Street,
London WC2B 5HH. Tel: 0171 240 1514
Fax: 0171 379 7493

Mr H Tartt
26 Baildon Street
Deptford
LONDON
SE8 4BQ

Wednesday, 15 December 1999

Dear Mr Tartt

Thank you for your letter concerning your recent visit to the Fortune Theatre and the Woman in Black.

Although I do not suffer from the 'delicate affliction' from which you suffer, on recent visits to Ute Lemper in Concert and Amy's View, I have been 'caught short' myself. Luckily, I have been able to distract myself enough to prevent a major catastrophe. However, how fortuitous of you to carry a spare pair of trousers.

As regards to the whereabouts of your cloth cap, I am afraid to report that no cap matching the description has been found.

I will try to find a way of warning elderly patrons, but, thus far, I have not been able to find the right words.

Would it be possible for me to reproduce your most eloquent letter in the next edition of our programme?

In anticipation

Yours sincerely

Andrew Jenkins
Theatre Manager

VAT No: 341 1878 62
Registered in England No: 1652164
Registered Address: 10 London Mews, W2 1HY

26 Baildon Street
Deptford
London SE8 4bq.

Fortune Theater
Russell Street
London WC2B 5HH.

Dear Andrew,

Thank you for your letter, it is a shame about the cap - but it isnt the first one I've lost. With regards my letter, if it can save just one poor old soul the embarrasment and humiliation I went through, then I think its a good idea to put it in your program. I also want to say that the lady who attended with me, Mrs. Mkobi, enjoyed the show very much - she kept clinging to me for comfort, which was loveley. In fact, it was her scream that caused me to have my accident (but she wasnt to know).

On condition of you printing before-mentioned letter - could you send me a copy of said program? It would make a lovely memento of what was (trouser expereince apart) a very fine evening.

Many thanks, and sorry about the seat.

Harry Tartt. Pensioner.

26 Baildon Street
Deptford
London SE8 4BQ.

Resource Library
Deptford Town Hall
New Cross Road
London Se14.

Dear Sir or madam,

I beleive you have lots of records of Deptford and such like, well, I wonder if you have a photo (I beleive it was printed in the old Kentish Mercury) of my uncles being ejected in 1929 from the old Empire. They was a music-hall act known as The Tumbling Tartts, and Max Miller once referred to them as "the most dangerous men in music hall". Supposedley thair act was very good, but they let themselfs down as people.

the chronicle also printed a photo of my dad bravely driving Alby Goldmans' van at the Brown Shirts on Cable Street. According to dad, as he drove off he heard Alby scream "Not the bloody truck Stanley!" Sure enough it was set ablaze within minutes and my dad had to fight off the facists with a bread stick.

Do you have photos of either event? I'd be most gratefull to you.

Yours hopefully,

Harry Tartt.

Magpie Resource Library,
Deptford Town Hall,
New Cross Road,
London SE14 6AF
Tel: 0171 919 7046
info@magpiecrl.org.uk

Magpie
Resource Library

encouraging local participation in
planning, regeneration, heritage
and environmental protection.

Harry Tartt,
26 Baildon Street,
Deptford,
London SE8 4BQ

22 January 2000.

PHOTOGRAPH COLLECTION:

Dear Mr Tartt,

Thanks for your fascinating letter, and I will try to find something for you.

Unfortunately I am only here half-time, and we still have a lot of work to do on sorting and indexing our picture archives.
Many of the photos that we have received are still in separate collections, each organised in its own way, so it will take me a little while to check through each one.

Yesterday I came in to find another large consignment of photos and slides had just arrived from Lewisham Council and the former Deptford City Challenge – in fact enough to fill half a filing cabinet – all of which needs to be filed away somehow.

I will be in touch as soon as I have found something relevant, and I will also try to suggest other archive sources that may be able to help.

Yours sincerely,

Alan Piper,
Librarian/ Co-ordinator.

Collections/ Tartt enqy.doc

A partnership project between Deptford History Group, Deptford Community Forum and Goldsmiths College
(Professional and Community Education)
Registered Charity No. 1070150
The library service is funded by the National Lottery Charities Board.

26 Baildon Street
Deptford
London Se8 4BQ/

Dear Bill Giles,

I used to be a big fan of yours but was recentley disturbed to read that you bullied the
other weathermen. I happen to be a big fan of Ian mcGaskill and I sinserely hope you
dont pick on him. I dont really care about Michael Fish (I find him a little oily).
Besides, I'm sure the article was all codswollop (they print anything these days!) I'm
sorry to have bought it up actually. Anyway, I've always enjoyed your weather
reports, you're the best. Keep up the good work.
Could you send me a photo?

All the best now,

Harry Tartt.

The Met.Office

BBC Weather Centre
BBC Television Centre Room 2027
Wood Lane London W12 7RJ

Tel: +44 (0)181 225 7769
Fax: +44 (0)181 749 2864

Harry Tartt
26 Baildon Street
Deptford
London SE8 4BQ

14th December 1999

Dear Harry

Thank you for your letter to Bill Giles which has been passed to me for reply.

I have pleasure in enclosing a photograph of Bill Giles and thank you for showing your interest.

Yours sincerely

Daksha Tailor
BBC Weather Centre

To Harry
Bill Giles.

26 Baildon Street
Deptford
London SE8 4bQ

Dear Tony Benn,

I want to start off by telling you that I used to be violentley opposed to everything you stood for. That apart though, I think that the House of Commons will be a poorer place without you. Still, us old political animals have been put out to pasture now havent we? But looking back I can say that I miss the old cut and thrust of political debate - harranging you whenever and wherever you spoke (perhaps you remember Eric Heffer wrestling me to the ground in Trafalgar Square?).

Times have changed now though, I have been allocated a "link-worker", if you please. A young berk called Steve who comes round once a week, asks if Im alright, watches Countdown, then leaves. It's madness. Mind you, I have lateley learnt that people can turn over a new leaf - young Kenny Pringle (who used to terrorise the estate) now does my shopping for me. A couple of times, if I cant make it down the pub, Ive even had him round for a drink and a chat. He's as good as gold actualy.

Perhaps Im just mellowing with age, hey?

Please send a christmas greeting to your old enemy,

Harry tartt.

Mr Harry Tartt
26 Baildon St
Deptford
London SE8 4BQ

6 December 1999

From Tony Benn

Dear Harry Tartt,

Just a line to thank you for your letter and to wish you all the best for Christmas and the New
Year.

With best wishes,

Tony Benn

26 Baildon Street
Deptford
London SE8 4Bq.

William Hill Customer Relations
Greenside House
50 Station Road,
Wood Green,
London N22 4Tp.

Dear Sir or miss,

Can you tell me - is it possible to lay a bet on weather the world will end on December 31st 1999?

The reason I ask is Mrs. Mkobi at the local cornershop reckons it will. 1, however, don't. What are the odds?

Yours faithfully,

Mr. Harry Tartt.

Greenside House, 50 Station Road, Wood Green, London N22 7TP
Telephone: 020 8918 3600

Mr H. Tartt,
26 Baildon Street,
Deptford,
London.   SE8 4BQ.

18th November 1999

Dear Mr Tartt,

Mrs Mkobi has a point and if, indeed the world is to come to an end I suggest stocking up with goodies in order to fortify oneself for the trip to eternity.

Of course there will probably be bookies in Heaven, and there definitely will be in Hell, so in the event that one should win a bet on the date of the end of the world it will be possible to collect winnings in the Hereafter.

I can offer you whatever odds you would like to name about the world ending on December 31st, 1999.

Yours sincerely,

Graham Sharpe
Media Relations Manager

William Hill Organization Limited. Registered Office: Greenside House,
50 Station Road, Wood Green, London N22 7TP. Reg. No. 278208 England

26 Baildon Street
Deptford
London SE8 4BQ.

William Hill Customer Relations
Greenside House
50 Station Road
Wood Green
London N22 4TP.

Dear Mr. Sharpe,

Well, well, well, very "sharp" indeed - but maybe not sharp enough - because correct me if Im wrong (and Im not), but what I asked for in my letter to you was odds on the world _not_ ending on December 31st 1999. So, acording to you I can have whatever odds I want. I would therefore like 10/1 on the world _not_ ending on this date.

I trust you are a man of honor.

Yours awaiting a reply,

Mr. Harry Tartt.

Greenside House, 50 Station Road, Wood Green, London N22 7TP
Telephone: 020 8918 3600

Mr H. Tartt,
26 Baildon Street,
Deptford,
London.   SE8 4BQ.

13th December 1999

Dear Mr Tartt,

Thank you for your letter.

A close reading of your original correspondence reveals that you asked "is it possible to lay a bet on weather (sic) the world will end on December 31st, 1999?"

Your second letter asked for odds of "10/1 on" about "the world not ending" on December 31st, 1999.

Any bet struck at odds of 10/1 on would, after deductions, return a profit of 1p for every £10 staked.

If you wish to place such a bet - for £10 - I will take it.

Yours sincerely,

Graham Sharpe
Media Relations Manager

26 Baildon STReet
Deprtford
London Se8 4BQ.

William Hill Customer Realations
Greenside House

50 Station Road,
Wood Green
London N22 4TP.

Dear Graham Sharpe,

I have to say I am suprised that you can only offer 1p on £10 steaked. Well, as a matter of honor I am going to place a £10 bet. Mrs. Mkobi thinks Im being silly, but she doesnt understand men. I have enclosed my wager which I trust will soon be winging its way back to me. I hope you realise that the only way you can wriggle out of this mr. sharpe, is if the world ends, and that for you, would be a hollow victory indeed.

Please find enclosed a postal order for £10.

Yours sincereley,

Mr. Harry tartt.

26 Baildon Street
Deptford
LONDON SE8 4BQ.

Dear Roger Daltrey,

At first I must admit, I used to deplore your early shenanighans, but now I have a respect for what youve done. I have never condoned robbing banks and post-offices with sawn-off shot-guns - but the fact that you did go and get a degree in Social Studies does offer some hope to the young boys who have gone off the rails. I am thinking of one in particular, a young Kenny Pringle, who luckily now seem s to be back on track. In fact it was him that showed me the film of your life - "McVicar".

Could you please send a signed photo made out to Kenny, as it might just serve to keep him on track.

Cheers now,

Harry tartt.

NO REPLY.

26 Baildon Street
deptford
London Se8 4BQ.

Dear john Altman and June Brown (alias Dot and Nick Cotton),

Hello and welcome to Lewisham on behalf of me and all the regulars of The Angry Toad (excepting Billy Baxter, whos a miserable so-and-so). I have been a big fan of you both for donkeys years, but unfortunately I wont be able to attend your production of Peter Pan at Lewisham Theatre - as I am a senior citizen and cant afford it. So I wonder if you could send me a nice photo of you both in costume. Perhaps John could write something sinister? ("Hello Ma!")

I know youll both be busy what with make-up and that, but before I go June, I have a story that might amuse you. A good few years back at the self same theatre an enraged Antony Newley, mid-perfOrmance, jumped off the stage and chased me out of the auditoriumn. He very nearley caught up with me on Catford High Street, but as luck would have it I managed to jump aboard a passing 36b. I'm not sure but I think he was on the juice at the time, post -Joan Collins and all that. It was only later that I learnt what had given him the hump - apparentley whenever he hit a certain note, my hearing aid would let off a deafening high-pitched sound. He must have thought I was doing it on purpose!

The funny thing being, I was.

Anyway, look forward to your photo. Break a leg.

Harry Tartt.

12.12.99.

Catford Theatre
Lewisham
Box Office
0181 690 0002.

Dear Harry,

Please see the pantomime at John's & my expense! Book yourself 2 tickets for which performance you want and I will inform them at the Box Office that they will be paid for by us.

Happy Christmas,

June Brown

x

JUNE BROWN
as ... Cotton

"for Harry"

BBC Copyright ©
Printed by New Perspectives 020-8440 5515

13.12.99

JOHN ALTMAN
as Nick Cotton

Agent: Roger Carey Associates 0171-630 6301

Photograph by Nicholas Bowman (1998)

26 Baildon Street
Deptford London
SE8 4BQ.

Dear John Altman and June Brown

He's behind you! Oh no he isnt!!
Joking apart though - it was very kind of you to offer me tickets for youre panto - a
lovely gesture indeed. Unfortunateley I'm going to have to decline due to a very busy
scedule, but I cherish the offer I realy do. You see, in the run-up to Christmas Im off
up to Cardiff to visit my old pal Taffy Edwards, and for Old Years Night, Mrs.
Mkobi's invited me home to meet meet her family. At first I thought she meant in
Africa, so I asked what I should do about jabs, she replied "jabs are optional, they live
in Neesdon!" She's a real live one. Sinse I've met her Ive become a new man - I've
already knocked the cigs on the head and my New Years resolution is to smile more.
If I receive half the kindness of the sort you showed, that shouldnt be too hard.

Good luck to you both, the world would be a better place if every one showed your
kindness.

Lots of love,

#

Harry Tartt.

P.S. Your lovely gesture certainly helps put Mr. Newleys actions into perspective.

26 Baildon street
Deptford
London SE8 4BQ.

Dear Jeffrey Archer,

I was very sorry to see you stiched-up in the run-up to Mayor. Your wit, drive, and ready-charm would have been a real tonic to us Londoners. I am also disturbed lest Red Ken gets in through the back-door. Still, you are a survivor Mr. Archer, a real slugger who can take the ocasional sock to the chin, not like the rest of these glass-jawed fly-weights. Rest assured you have the respect and loyalty of all the regulars at The Angry Toad in Deptford (excepting Alfie Crum who used to be a Communist). Good luck Sir, and keep ducking and diving.

Harry tartt.

P.S. Could you send a Christmas greeting to me and Mrs. Nkomi?

MERRY CHRISTMAS
&
A HAPPY NEW YEAR

Jeffrey Archer

Greenside House, 50 Station Road, Wood Green, London N22 7TP
Telephone: 0181 918 3600

With Compliments

Congratulations -
Don't spend all your
winnings at once

William Hill Organization Limited. Registered Office: Greenside House,
50 Station Road, Wood Green, London N22 7TP. Reg. No. 278208 England